PUT YOUR WORST FOOT FORWARD

As the first Mentee in HEMP, I feel like I won the lottery; and in many, many ways, I did. It's very likely that I would not have made it without Barnett, my Mentor, Henry Bloch, and the rest of the HEMP community.

In early 1995, I was out of gas, out of money, and nearly out of hope. HEMP was the best thing that ever happened to me, and I drank the "Kool-Aid" from the first day. Talking about the issues facing your company was never a problem for me, so the saying "Put Your Worst Foot Forward" was totally natural; and transformative.

With Barnett's help, we formed an advisory board, and for the next 25 years, we focused on any and all things standing in the way of success.

I loved Henry Bloch in the same way I love Barnett, just like my dad. This book and the pearls it contains can transform your life as well as your company. Read it, live it – your team and family will be happy that you did.

Danny O'Neill
Founder, The Roasterie, Inc.

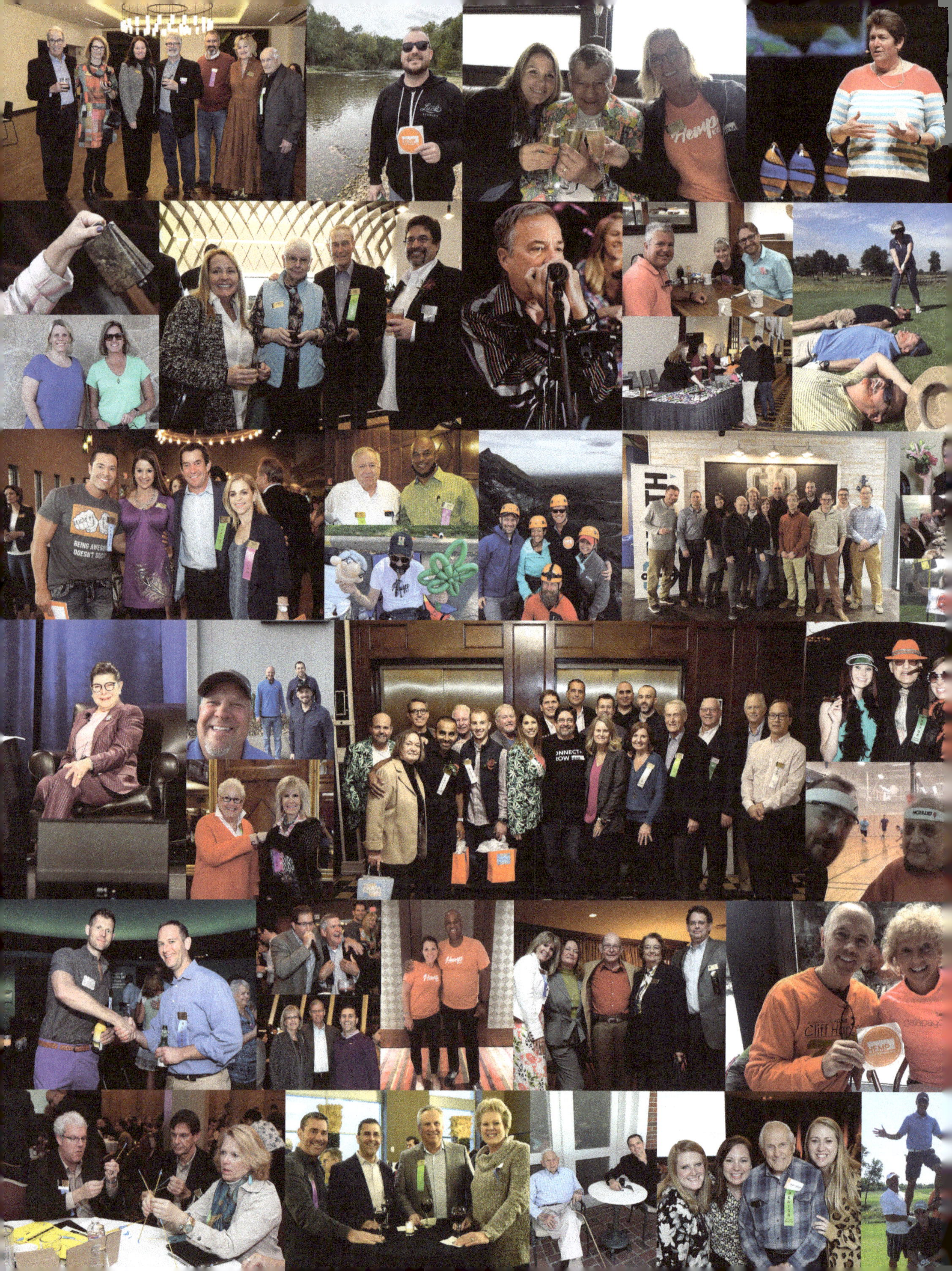

PUT YOUR WORST FOOT FORWARD

Twenty-Five Years of Growing the Helzberg Entrepreneurial Mentoring Program

Barnett C. Helzberg, Jr.
Maureen Rank, Tracy Lockton, and Christina Dreiling

For more information, contact:

MISSION POINT PRESS

Mission Point Press
2554 Chandler Road
Traverse City, Michigan 49696
www.MissionPointPress.com
(231) 421-9513

Edited by Meredith Reynolds, Darlene Short and Sharon Silva
Designed by Haley Young

Printed in the United States of America

Softcover ISBN: 978-1-958363-00-3
Hardcover ISBN: 978-1-958363-07-2

Library of Congress Control Number: 2022909776

For Mom
Thank you for your unlimited
love and example of the
beauty of reading
and learning. I miss and
love you daily.

For Dad
Thank you for your love and your
wisdom. I quote you constantly
and always follow your advice.
You made us look at all the pluses
when the challenges came, and I
am forever grateful.

For Shirley
Thank you for your support of me, my idea, and this program
from day one. I have always considered you the eighth wonder of the world.
People ask me, "Does your wife ever sleep?" More important, you have been
so good to me in so many ways and changed my life, so I thank you for being
you. Of course, I also appreciate how you have always backed me when
people have said my ideas were undoable.
My love forever, from the luckiest person in the world.

For Tracy Lockton and Christina Dreiling
A very special thank you to you both. This book would not have
been possible—or completed—without you. Thank you for all your hard work
in the making of HEMP and this book with me!

CONTENTS

FOREWORD

I have been a Mentor in the Helzberg Entrepreneurial Mentoring Program (HEMP) since 2012, served as the chair of the Mentor Committee, participated in other committees, and am currently president of HEMP. It is the most unique professional organization in which I have been involved.

I am excited you are reading this book. You will not only learn about HEMP and how it has evolved but will also meet its founder and the book's author, Barnett C. Helzberg, Jr. Barnett is adamant about not taking too much credit for the creation and success of HEMP. But the truth is, he has authentically led and motivated us while personally attracting all the high-performing professionals who give their time, wisdom, passion, and experience to the organization. I don't want to give up the secret sauce you will read about in the following pages, but I do want to share a few things you won't find that are key ingredients in our recipe for success.

Barnett has led HEMP with his presence and personal philosophies. His interaction with everyone in the organization creates the standard for the rest of us to follow. A great example is the true respect and admiration that he and Christina Dreiling, our managing director, have developed over the seventeen years they have worked together. This relationship has fostered some behaviors that they probably don't even recognize as valuable elements, but that our participants witness whenever they are in our office, at a meeting, or at an event. Their thoughtful conduct is present in how they speak to each other and to everyone else in the room. This caring style combined with humor and fun spills over into everyone else's behavior. It is infectious and a wonderful undertone that permeates our organization. The warmth and trust evident in their relationship has set the norm for all others to follow.

The way that Christina and her fellow employees, Haley Young and Maggie Johnson, set up a room for both business and social events helps HEMPers know they are welcome and in a safe place—a place to let their shoulders relax and to mingle easily with others they haven't seen in a while or are meeting for the first time. An observer will notice ready smiles, vigorous conversation, HEMP coffee mugs with freshly brewed Roasterie coffee, green smoothies (our signature "Kool-Aid," as we call it), and plenty of everyone's favorite chocolate-covered roasted peanuts. Our budget will always include these "little" things.

We have had people outside of HEMP comment on our unique organization culture. One of our speakers, CEO Chet Cadieux of QuikTrip, told us he had never spoken to such an engaged group. He watched our crowd before the event began and didn't see a single person on a cell phone. Everyone was up talking with others, and our speaker could feel the electric HEMP energy.

There have been many times when Barnett or Christina has surprised me with a telephone call, a handwritten thank-you note, or a gift of appreciation. They make me feel special, appreciated, and valued. Of course, I am going to continue to donate my time! And I have no doubt that after reading this book, you will want to join us or will decide to create your very own passion project to support your community.

Tracy Lockton
HEMP President 2020

Barnett C. Helzberg, Jr. in his signature "HEMP jacket" posing in front of HEMP's event space, Barnett's Basement.

Meaning of the Mission

As I write, HEMP has been in business for twenty-five years. In that time, nearly eight hundred business leaders and the companies they lead have been part of this experience. I'm still trying to understand why we've arrived at this point and, frankly, how we made some pretty good things happen. After thinking about this a great deal, I have come to these conclusions:

"Thank You" cookies for Scott King after his term as HEMP President.

1 We've very, very carefully chosen the right individuals to be part of the team. Each new participant was selected based on strong criteria and only after a great deal of agonized decision-making.

2 You've probably come across the quote, "Being listened to is so close to being loved that most people cannot tell the difference." Both our Mentees and Mentors listen with this philosophy, and perhaps it has helped prolong our organizational success.

3 A mutual vulnerability can create a bond. Whether you are the Mentor or the Mentee, putting your worst foot forward to the other creates some special magic, especially when this is backed up by the pledge of absolute confidentiality.

At this time, as HEMP hits its twenty-fifth anniversary, I am asking myself some questions: How will HEMP endure? What are the nonnegotiable values that make this organization what it is? How can we embed them deeply and enduringly enough so when we "founders" have gone to our reward, HEMP goes on, true to mission? Those questions—and their answers—are why we created this book.

We want you to know where HEMP came from so the meaning of the mission makes sense. And we want you to see how it grew so the thinking behind some of the programs and systems that define it can be maintained, adjusted, or reinvented inside the filter of the mission and values that make the organization unique.

> **There's no good writing, only good rewriting.**

Shirley Bush Helzberg and Barnett C. Helzberg, Jr. smile under their masks at the 2020 HEMP Drive-Thru Retreat.

HEMP has been, without question, one of the great experiences of my life. When people have said that I've been generous, I have explained to them, "I am not generous. I am selfish. I could be hanging out with my contemporaries hearing about their new hips and knees, or I can be spending time with these amazing entrepreneurs." Through this program, I have met many wonderful people I would never have known. Hopefully, in some cases, we have helped them both attain success and do more for their associates in financial terms. Also, there have been interesting cases where Mentees felt we played a part in personal growth. I think of the story of a Mentee whose Mentor's first assignment for him was to take his wife on a date. His Mentor explained that you must have your house in order because it carries over into your work.

It's important to mention the names of the women and men who have given their time (and I mean *given*, since only a handful of team members get paid). I want you to understand that HEMP is what it is because of its participants and the brainpower, business acumen, and passion that together have created a resource for business success we hope lasts for another 25 years and beyond. Please recognize that I cannot begin to mention everyone, but *everyone* is important and has a special place in my heart.

My incredible wife, Shirley, is my earliest backer and worked beside me to transform my idea into a reality. Shirley is a devoted patron of Kansas City and has worked tirelessly for our arts community. Her years of service include chairing the boards of the Nelson-Atkins Museum of Art and the Starlight Theatre, eighteen years as head of the Kansas City Symphony board, and support for countless other institutions and causes. Shirley has redeveloped many old buildings in the Kansas City Crossroads area. I bring this up because Shirley's role model was the late Paul Henson, a pioneer in fiber optic phones. When Shirley shared with Paul what we were doing to create a mentoring program, Paul replied, "Do you know how big this could be?" Paul knew before we did how great HEMP could be. His positive response added credibility and excitement that stuck with Shirley and me.

Muggs Lorber, my beloved childhood camp director, told his young charges, "Always leave your campsite better than you found it." When I was twelve, I thought he was only referring to a campsite. As I got older, I began to understand that he was actually talking about the whole world. In my Jewish heritage, this idea is called *tikkun olam*, Hebrew for "repairing the world." Contributing to entrepreneurs' success and better lives for their associates through the Helzberg Entrepreneurial Mentoring Program has been an application of this wise philosophy.

I hope in reading this book you'll find some enjoyment, get at least one valuable idea, or pearl as we call them, and contribute more thoughts on mentoring by contacting HEMP at info@hempkc.org.

HEMPingly yours,
TBG *(you'll understand who this is later!)*

PUT YOUR WORST FOOT FORWARD

Part 1:
HEMP 2020

At every event, HEMPers are welcomed with a smile as they receive their name badge. Here, HEMP managing director, Christina Dreiling, greets HEMPers at Schmooze Fest 2008.

CHAPTER 1

Who We've Become

In 1995, I invited a group of business leaders to join me in helping others who wanted to succeed as we had. I had chosen to focus our help on a particular subset of entrepreneurs, those whose businesses had made it to second-stage growth. They had moved through the throes of start-up but hadn't yet fulfilled all their potential for success. The leaders who joined me came on board to help create a mentoring program designed especially for these second-stage entrepreneurs.

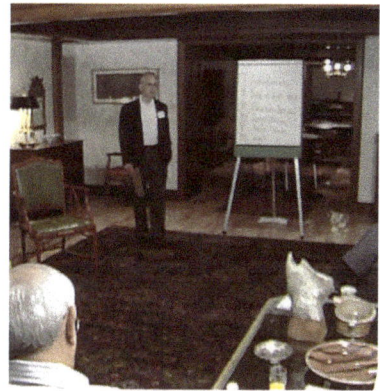

Harvey Thomas facilitates the discussion at HEMP's first meeting.

We identified ways our Mentors had helped us, such as pushing us via good listening and great questions to make our own decisions. We also defined what seemed to make someone "mentorable"—willing to ask for help and work with another toward a solution. From these very early discussions, the program took shape. Mentees were invited to learn, paired with Mentors, and conversations began.

Now, after a quarter century of practice, we know better how to support and even improve mentoring and how to find high-quality Mentees and Mentors.

HEMP is a lean machine currently run by our managing director, Christina Dreiling, who has been with us since 2003. We have been incredibly lucky to have her, not just because of her many talents that make her a strong leader but also because she has grown with our organization. Christina brings the knowledge and battle scars of history, the fond memories of all those who have gotten us to where we are today, and an endearing devotion to HEMP and all our HEMPers. I hope she is with us for twenty more years.

Over the twenty-five years of HEMP, nearly eight hundred businesses and their ultimate decision-makers have been helped by the investment of more than two hundred Mentors. And through the years, we've sharpened our interview, selection, training, and integration processes for these Mentor-Mentee combinations. But we've also added a beautiful wraparound of group- and peer-mentoring opportunities to be sure help is coming from all sides. This includes Tiger Teams, small groups that can come together in a matter of hours to provide help when urgent needs arise.

HEMP hosts twelve to twenty-four educational programs annually. We select top-quality, highly experienced presenters to bring business information our participants need to stay ahead of the curve on decisions and problem-solving. Our annual one-day retreat offers input from high-profile thought leaders like Steve Wozniak, cofounder of Apple, and Brené Brown, known globally for her work on vulnerability in business and life. The retreat is a chance for all our participants to come together and remember to work *on* the business, not *in* it.

HEMP retreat speaker Brené Brown.

We've also learned the power of what we call classes. The formal mentoring experience lasts three years. Mentees become part of not only a learning relationship but also a class of other Mentees who share a similar commitment to growing their businesses together at HEMP.

Currently, our guidelines for Mentee selection start by considering companies that have been in business for at least three years, have annual revenue of around $1 million or more, and have at least five full-time employees. The business owner must demonstrate a desire to grow, have a record of integrity, and provide sound financials. As a result, classes of Mentees come together with strong commonalities. Even if their industries differ—and we intend that they do—second-stage problems are similar. When classmates share issues and others respond, "Yes, I know what you mean," they do! Both ideas and camaraderie can flow, particularly crucial in the lonely and sometimes isolated role of leading a company. My folks always taught me that "Business is people," so building these relationships is crucial.

We continue to improve our interview questions and our selection process. After reviewing Mentee prospect applications, we select about three-fourths of them to conduct rigorous site visits and interviews. Security checks and references are carefully reviewed. Standards for entering the program continue to rise, so Mentees know their selection means they've joined a group of like-minded and similarly committed peers who do business the way they do.

Barnett C. Helzberg, Jr. with Steve Wozniak, cofounder of Apple, Inc. at HEMP's 20th Anniversary Celebration at the Kauffman Center for the Performing Arts.

The HEMP Class of 2020 catching up after a HEMP event.

The same is true for Mentors, as we find better ways to present both the advantages and expectations for those wanting to help others in this way. Mentors volunteer their time knowing they'll be expected to meet with their Mentees at least twice a month the first year and once a month the second and third years and attend at least 50 percent of HEMP's events annually. They take relief in knowing that we check with both them and their Mentees regularly to be sure the relationship is "jelling."

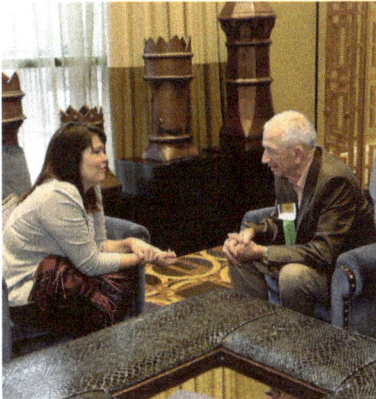

HEMP Fellow Haley Haar talks strategy with her Mentor, John Miller.

Please don't forget Mentors are highly successful businesspeople. That's what qualifies them to help in this program. And we're aware they have multiple requests pushing them to share their time and expertise. These are the people we boldly invite to volunteer, and then we turn around and insist on applications, interviews, behavioral assessments, and more from them before they are accepted as Mentors. (We often shake our heads in wonder that people would put themselves through all this when the only reward is the joy of contributing significantly to another's growth.)

Equally amazing is this: we quickly learned that once a part of this community of business learners, people don't want to leave! After finishing their stint as Mentees, participants would ask us about sticking around for the programs, the events, the relationships, and the one-of-a-kind community. Also, Mentors who weren't matched to a Mentee in a particular year asked how they might still participate. Other resource people who gave time to help in specialized areas, like finances or human resources, asked the same question.

From this interest, a new group called Fellows was created. This society currently numbers more than one hundred participants who meet regularly, take part in events, and help sustain HEMP financially.

Of course, being the results-driven business types we are, we would, in time, ask participants to quantify the help they were receiving. We have consistently learned that on average, a Mentee who completes the three-year HEMP mentoring experience increases business revenue by 43 percent and sees a 41 percent growth in her or his employee count. Across the city, we've estimated HEMP's total economic impact to be more than $748 million.

Just as powerful, and perhaps more so because we are a relationship-intense enterprise, is the feedback from participants, both Mentees and Mentors, about how the program has affected them (see pages 22 and 23).

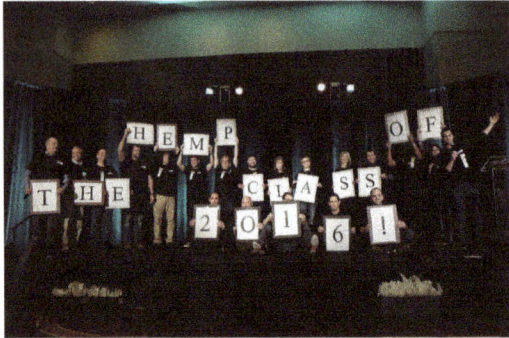

The HEMP Class of 2016 performs their class skit at the HEMP retreat, an annual tradition for the new Mentee class.

> It's like my Mentor is a trail guide. He hasn't necessarily been on the exact path I'm on, but he's done a lot of walking on similar paths. I feel so supported.

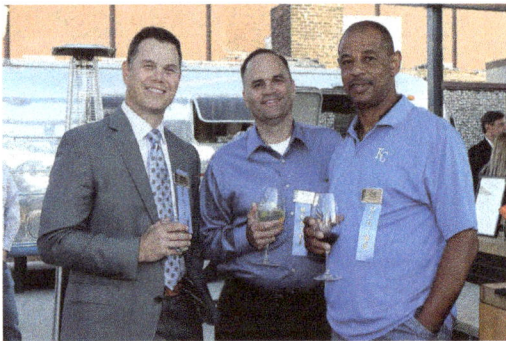

HEMP Fellows Mike Zimmerman, Kyle Batts, and Eric Burtin at a Celebrate HEMP event.

> My Mentor can see skills and abilities where others do not. She also has the talent to extract those skills in methods that fit the individual. She gave me courage and insight to do things I never thought possible.

> My Mentor is there as an ear and a voice - listening, testing, and encouraging. It's a friendship first but a mentorship nonetheless. After all, mentorship without friendship is just a job.

Austin Bickford with Barnett C. Helzberg, Jr. and his Mentor, Bob Brush.

> HEMP is a one-of-a-kind experience that is based on a shared passion for business success. At HEMP we learn together, and grow together, both personally and professionally. It is such a pleasure and an honor to be a part of this wonderful organization!

HEMP Fellows Susan Ahn, Courtney Thomas, Haley Haar, and Jennifer Juarez.

Mentor Testimonials

> Mentoring is really simple. It's not about what the Mentor knows; it is about helping the Mentee define and achieve his or her goals by listening.

Mentor Laura Lee Jones is cheered on by her Mentee, Karah Jones, at her boxing match.

> HEMP mentoring is personally fulfilling because it challenges me to be—without any self-interest—an informed, experienced, challenging listener with the best interest of the Mentee as my overriding concern.

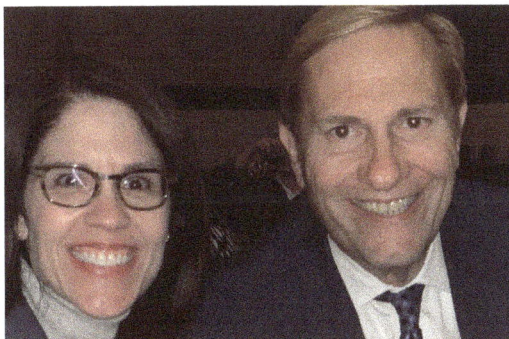

Laura Schmidt is all smiles with her Mentor, R. Lee Harris.

Rick Krska, Missy Love, Danny O'Neill, and Melody Warren reminisce about early retreats.

> You know you are succeeding as a Mentor when you can draw the answers to problems from the Mentees themselves.

Jay Tomlinson and his Mentor, Chuck Hoffman.

> But perhaps most powerful has been the creation of a community of mutually supportive business leaders. They are willing to be vulnerable with one another, maintain a commitment to strict confidentiality, and commit themselves without reservation—and to do it all with a healthy dose of fun.

HEMP's Rules of the Road

With the passage of time, things will change within HEMP, but we want to put our stake in the ground here to show you exactly what we are based on. I want to make it clear how we operate and where we came from so future observers will better understand who we are. This is our "conscience"—the inner voice that guides what's right and what's wrong as we make decisions and go about the work. Simply put, it is what we are most passionate about for HEMP. These are HEMP's Rules of the Road, our guidelines for selection and participation, administration, atmosphere, and priorities. In a few cases, I have included a personal story to illustrate how important a particular rule is for HEMP because people remember stories.

1 Mentor and Mentee quality must never be compromised.

2 Mentor and Mentee quality must never be compromised.

3 Mentor and Mentee quality must never be compromised. (This is not a typo. This rule is so important it needs to be repeated!)

4 Quality over quantity will drive the selection of Mentees. HEMP has always believed bigger isn't better; better is better. While HEMP needs a certain number of Mentees to be financially sustainable, it's essential to always choose for fit, not to fill a numerical goal.

Barnett Note

As my English teacher, Virginia Scott Minor, used to say, "When in doubt, leave it out." If there is a concern about selecting a specific candidate, err on the side of caution and don't select that person.

5 Mentees and Mentors must never be chosen because they have a personal relationship with another participant. Selection at HEMP must always be unbiased.

6 Participants must have no hidden agenda. To maintain the safe environment HEMP provides, they will never solicit business or charitable donations from other participants. If sought out by others interested in their product or service, however, they may respond.

7 Mentors will maintain their objectivity by never investing financially in the businesses of their Mentees. A Mentor must be influenced only by the Mentee's good.

8 HEMP will continue to commit to the needs of and identify specific programming for one of our most significant resources, our Fellows (Mentee graduates).

9 Problem participants who require a disproportionate amount of team members' time should be let go quickly. One Mentee overusing resources takes away from what all the others should be receiving.

10 The Resource Guide (HEMP's participant directory) is considered a sacred trust and can be used only by participants. It must never be shared with people outside of HEMP or within a participant's organization. When resource people do make themselves available, they will acknowledge the request and arrange to provide help within twenty-four hours. Prompt responses to one another are an understanding of all HEMPers.

11 Absolute confidentiality is a rule with no exceptions. When HEMPers have conversations, the information they share is always considered confidential. One must ask for permission before sharing what was learned with anyone else, whether you are the president of HEMP or a Mentee.

Barnett Note

I am proud that even Christina, our managing director, never shares information about Mentee conversations with others — and that includes me!

12 When asked, participants will, without hesitation, give honest and confidential evaluations of programs. The organization must be regularly and profoundly evaluated to find ways to do things better. In this spirit of continuous improvement, a survey to probe participants' thoughts and concerns is ideally conducted at least every five years.

13 Participation may be terminated by the participant or the organization at any time for any or no reason. If any participant is behaving unethically, the termination will be immediate.

14 The HEMP staff must be compensated fairly and treated with respect. A participant who disrespects or mistreats a staffer will be dismissed from the program.

15 HEMP's Restricted Reserve Fund for financial sustainability must have Executive Committee permission to be used, and only when absolutely necessary. It will not be used as a regular operating fund. Also, the twenty-year fund Barnett will be leaving HEMP once he goes to his reward will not be a guaranteed endowment, as endowments don't guarantee adherence to a mission.

Barnett Note

After observing a college endowment managed in ways that reduced it from $48 million to $28 million, I determined the same thing would not happen at HEMP. Therefore, for my part, I've created an "indirect endowment" so my family will make an annual decision about continuing support, honoring the donor intent. We believe this will provide some accountability for future leaders to HEMP's mission of bringing mentoring to second-stage business leaders.

16 HEMP's preference is for meetings, interviews and events to be eyeball-to-eyeball. When people are in real-time conversations, connections are created, and pearls of wisdom emerge. That's when the real magic happens.

17 HEMP's unique culture must always be cultivated. These four Spirits of The Big Guy should mark all HEMP experiences: Put Your Worst Foot Forward, Absolute Confidentiality, We Want Your "Soul," and Keep HEMP Fun!

18 Every decision must be filtered through its impact on HEMP's primary customers, the Mentees. Always ask, "Does it help Mentees?"

19 HEMP's growth will happen slowly and carefully. As noted in Rule 4, bigger isn't better; better is better.

20 HEMP will stay focused in Kansas City. It was created to build the Kansas City business community. The organization will offer help to mentoring organizations in other cities, but only if doing so doesn't compromise with original intent.

These are HEMP's Rules of the Road in 2020. We often share other important nuggets of advice on a regular basis that aren't as crucial for the sustainability of HEMP but should still be noted. Our HEMPers have lovingly coined the term, Barnettisms, because I drive them home so often.

Barnettisms

Always Have Two Suppliers
Your bank might change its mind. Your supplier might burn down or go out of business. Protect yourself!

Associates are Number One, Not Customers
Everything emanates from your people. If you treat your associates well, they will treat your customers well.

Be "Open Kimono"
You share the good news and the bad news. Especially the bad news before rumors get around making things look much worse than they are.

Boil the Rat
A rat can be boiled if you put it in water and raise the temperature one degree at an hour. Similarly with pricing, if you make very small increases annually it usually will not upset and cause the loss of customers, whereas it would if you wait 10 years and increase the price significantly.

Never be a Victim
Don't say, "poor me." Say, "Where do I go from here to be successful?"

Nobody is Smart All Over
Your most brilliant friend is not an expert on everything.

Value Output, Not Input
If you are on the phone all day with your daughter, but the work is getting done, why am I complaining?

Why Do I Keep Working With You?
Don't waste your Mentor's time or your time by meeting without activity.

You Ain't Nothing to Nobody if You Try to Be Everything to Everybody
You can't do everything, so you have to determine what you are the best at.

Now, come along to discover how it all unfolded. Then join us in celebrating twenty-five years of learning and in sharing our dreams for more ahead.

Mentors Tracy Lockton and Dave Lockton celebrating HEMP with Dr. Ryan Powell.

Part 2: Planting HEMP

(1995–1996)

Barnett C. Helzberg, Jr. shaking hands with Warren Buffett, chairman and CEO of Berkshire Hathaway.

CHAPTER 2

Mapping Out a Course

The spark that results in a new venture can come in a thousand different ways. For me, the inspiration for HEMP was perhaps akin to the middle-aged couple who, with their kids just off to college, decide to start a second family.

I had invested the first thirty-nine years of my work life building the family business, Helzberg Diamonds. It had grown from a fifteen-unit endeavor to, at that time, 143 stores and the third-largest jewelry retailer in twenty-three states. I was ready for a change and so was the business; I felt it had outgrown me. There were possibilities for expansion, but business for me is intensely personal. I couldn't stomach the thought of our family's reputation attached to people with whom I had no potential for a relationship.

The historic Helzberg Diamonds storefront formerly located on the Kansas City Country Club Plaza.

At that point, four things mattered to me: I wanted the business to continue to be headquartered in Kansas City. The current employees needed to stay on. It must not be sold to anyone who would simply sell it again to turn a quick profit. And finally, the business must not go public. (I felt so strongly about not going public that I included a chapter explaining the rationale in my book *What I Learned Before I Sold to Warren Buffett*.)

We began exploring options under the direction of financial services firm Morgan Stanley, which found many parties with an interest in buying the company. But there was one buyer I dreamed of: Warren Buffett.

I was aware that many companies shared this dream of selling to the best investor in the world. However, I wasn't all that focused on whether he'd want us, but rather on why we wanted him. I had purchased four shares of Buffett's company, Berkshire Hathaway, in 1989 so I could attend the annual meeting and learn from the best. In the years that followed, it became clear to me that our thinking about what made a company great and deeply lasting aligned with Berkshire Hathaway's. I knew we could trust Mr. Buffett to keep the headquarters in Kansas City, resist changing the company's character, and retain the jobs of all the Helzberg's associates. When I heard him say things like "Great people do great things," my dream solidified because it reminded me of my folks' words, "Business *is* people."

How to approach him? As it happened, the "moment of approach" came to me. I was in New York City meeting with our financial advisors at Morgan Stanley about the future of the company. As I walked past the Plaza Hotel on my way to the meeting, I heard a woman's voice call out, "Warren Buffett!" As I turned to look, the woman had just engaged in conversation with a man in an off-the-rack suit and a kind smile. Yep. Warren Buffett. Their discussion turned out to be a brief "hello" from a stockholder, and as they parted company, I saw my moment and stepped toward him, hand thrust out. "Mr. Buffett, I'm Barnett Helzberg of Helzberg Diamonds in Kansas City." And right there on the sidewalk, I took the next thirty seconds to tell him why he should buy our jewelry business.

"I believe our company matches your criteria for investment," I concluded. To which he replied, "Send me the information."

I would learn later he rarely took these approaches very seriously. Everyone running a lemonade stand wanted Berkshire Hathaway to own his enterprise, so Mr. Buffett had learned to keep his expectations low. But when I sent our numbers, he called to talk.

Soon we were in his office in Omaha negotiating a sale. I knew I would live with joy for a long time remembering what Buffett told shareholders about the acquisition. He said, "We associate ourselves with some real jewels of the American business world. And I think it's quite fitting that Helzberg joins this collection of jewels. It's got outstanding management. It's got a leadership position. It's on the move. I would hate to compete with you, fellows; I'd rather be on your side of the fence."

So, now what?

Here I was sixty years old and a poor candidate for retirement since I'm a guy who never much liked golf. My dynamo life partner, Shirley, had already jumped with both feet into growing the arts in Kansas City as chair of the board of the Nelson-Atkins Museum of Art and of the Kansas City Symphony and working for about thirty other causes. An aggressive pace had been set for me! It wasn't a question of whether to invest somewhere new but rather where to invest. What did I care about? Who needed what I could offer? (I remember telling people, "I'm not retiring *from* something; I'm retiring *to* something." But I wasn't sure what the something was going to be.)

The seed idea of how to give had already been planted years before. It came from a man who enriched my life and the work of entrepreneurs across the globe: Ewing Marion Kauffman.

Shirley and Barnett C. Helzberg, Jr.

Above: **Ewing Marion Kauffman**

One day I asked Mr. Kauffman, "How can I ever thank you?" He replied, "That's okay. You'll help somebody someday."

Although we both lived in Kansas City, I met Ewing Kauffman back in 1972 when he was the featured speaker at a seminar at Pebble Beach, California. This conference always provided speakers with top-notch credentials and experience. Still, in my book, they had outdone themselves by securing Ewing Kauffman.

He was impressive by anyone's standards. After leaving work as a pharmaceutical salesman in 1950, he took the entrepreneurial plunge and started his own pharmaceutical company in his basement. At the end of the first year, he had realized a net profit of a whopping $1,000. Almost forty years later, he sold Marion Laboratories, then a globally diversified healthcare giant, to Merrell Dow as a company with nearly $1 billion in sales and thirty-four hundred associates. But I think he was proudest of the fact that with the sale he created two hundred millionaires, many of whom would go on to become successful entrepreneurs.

Ewing Marion Kauffman at a speaking event.

The man knew how to grow a business. But he also understood how to build community spirit and how to develop others.

In 1968, he purchased a baseball franchise and created the Kansas City Royals, invigorating his home community with new pride and an income stream. His other deep and lasting contribution came in the form of the Ewing Marion Kauffman Foundation, now a global leader in developing entrepreneurs and education in underserved communities.

But the day I heard him speak, I was most impressed with his grace and humility. His wife introduced him to the audience and provided an entirely true but lengthy recounting of his successes. It must have embarrassed Mr. Kauffman a little because when he took the podium, he gave a slight nod to his wife, a wink to us, and said, "Now that you know Mrs. Kauffman, you understand my problems," and they laughed together.

After the talk, I invited him to meet for a drink. The conversation that followed must have worked for both of us because as we parted, he said, "Drop by the office when you get back to town."

His acceptance of that invitation for a drink started a twenty-three-year relationship that, in so many ways, aided my business success. Mr. K shared information and access to any resources he had. Most important, he knew how to ask the questions that made me discover answers for myself.

❝ Why do I keep working with you? Because you listen. ❞

Mr. Kauffman passed away in 1993, two years before Helzberg Diamonds became part of the Berkshire Hathaway family of companies. Although he was gone, his quiet words about "helping somebody someday" must have taken root. Two years before selling the family company, I experimented with ideas of how I could be useful. I asked people whose opinions I valued, such as the head of the Small Business Administration in Kansas City, about the idea of starting a mentoring organization to help entrepreneurs.

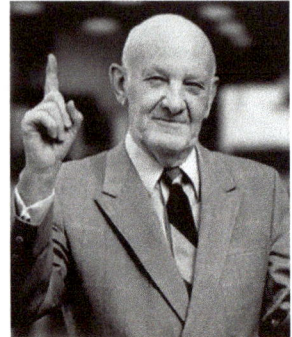

Ewing Marion Kauffman

I imagined some collection of one-to-one relationships taking place in a setting of useful business programs like I'd seen in other organizations. It would also have the kind of "safe place" that business owners need. When you lead a company, there are few people you can approach or places you can go to ask openly for help. Who are you going to turn to if you can't figure out some of your challenges? Employees, whose livelihoods depend on your venture, need to see you as having some semblance of competence. Competitors would love to know your struggles; it might open doors of opportunity! The idea would be to offer help, but safely given in the way Mr. Kauffman and various leadership organizations had been safe havens for me.

HEMP founding Mentor Chuck Hoffman

Responses to a letter inviting feedback were mixed. Some could see the value. But others, like longtime business friend and fishing buddy Chuck Hoffman, were sure the idea wouldn't work. "Why would successful businesspeople want to give their time away like this?" he pushed. "You're not paying them. What's in it for them?" (Chuck became the ninth president of HEMP, so clearly, he changed his mind. He has been an excellent Mentor, often helping Mentees who presented especially unusual challenges.)

Friend Morton Sosland, a significant leader in the Kansas City publishing industry, introduced the other major question. The anchor of my mentoring plan was personal chemistry because it was that chemistry and caring that had made the difference in my relationship with Mr. Kauffman. But how would you orchestrate chemistry? It's not a box to check or an item on an application to complete. Chemistry, like love, is either there or it isn't. It can be nourished but not demanded.

There was wisdom in the points made by both men. These very questions were part of why I spent two years *not* trying out the idea! However, whether intended or not, their reluctances encouraged my determination; we'd find a way to make it work.

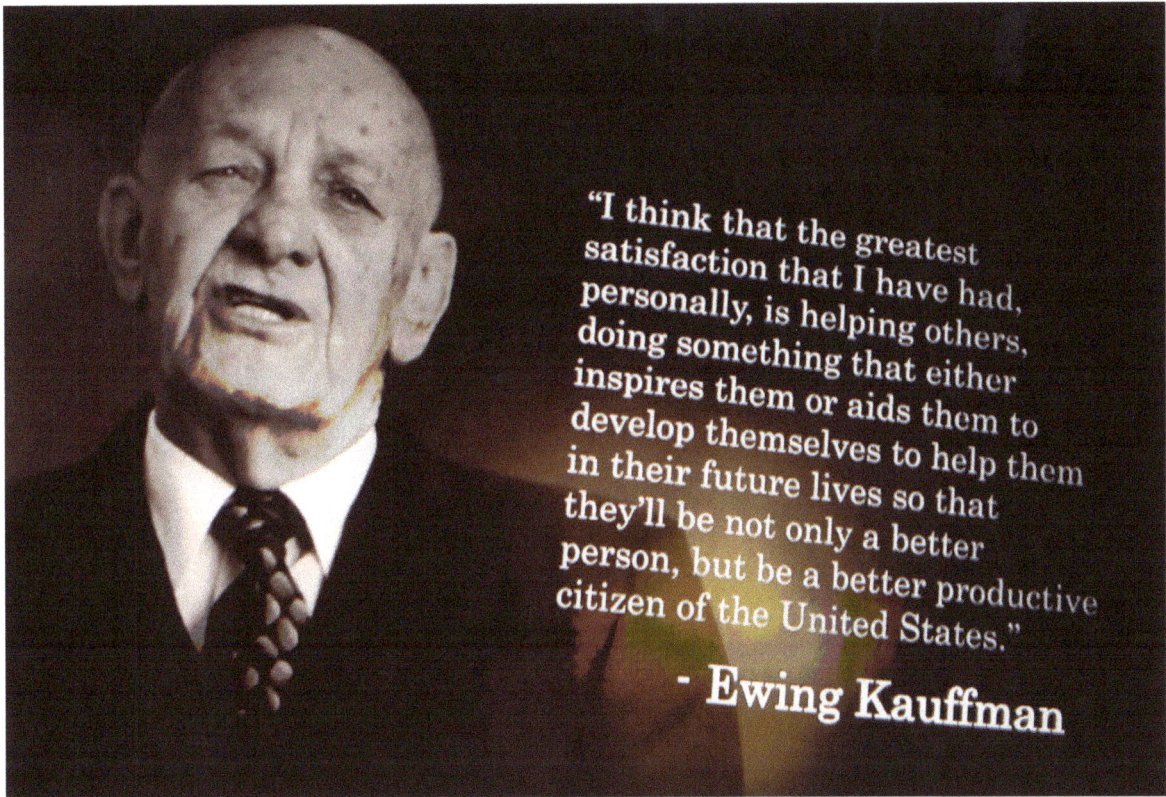

"I think that the greatest satisfaction that I have had, personally, is helping others, doing something that either inspires them or aids them to develop themselves to help them in their future lives so that they'll be not only a better person, but be a better productive citizen of the United States."

- Ewing Kauffman

But it took a verbal kick in the pants to move me to action. One day, after all this mental marinating, I was having lunch with Bill Eddy, dean of the Bloch School of Management at the University of Missouri–Kansas City (UMKC), and two of his colleagues, Bill French, vice chancellor for university advancement at UMKC, and Rich Davis, a child psychiatrist, creator of KC Masterpiece Barbecue Sauce, and a UMKC board member. They intended to ask if I would chair a gala to benefit the university. I knew if they wanted the world's worst choice for the job, they had made the correct pick. I can't hear, I talk too much, I'm a loose cannon, I don't prepare, and I can't sit, other than that, I'm the perfect candidate. I have always considered committee work the definition of cruel and unusual punishment. I declined the invitation, hopefully graciously.

The conversation somehow morphed into informal brainstorming, and future HEMP president Bill Eddy offered, "Maybe you could start a mentoring program." At that moment, Mr. Kauffman's quiet suggestion to "help someone someday" and two years of conversational exploration fused into a brain click. The next morning as I was shaving, I looked in the mirror and said to myself, "Look, Helzberg. Put up or shut up! It's time to stop bothering people all over town about this idea. Either do it or don't!"

That commitment marked HEMP's beginning.

Imagining the Benefits

The idea generated; the commitment made. I was now in new territory. The diamond business I had led was created by my grandfather and developed by my dad. I stepped in to grow it, not to start it. Like most fledgling entrepreneurs, I stumbled around. However, to my advantage, I've always known I'm no complex thinker; whoever invented the motto "Keep It Simple, Stupid" had likely bumped into me somewhere along the line. Plus, I'm an idea guy, not an execution guy. I realized I would need to focus high level, or the idea would drown in a sea of how-to details I wasn't equipped to manage.

After thirty-nine years in business, I knew success in this latest pursuit boiled down to three things: we would need great mentors, we would need great mentees, and we would need a way to get mentors and mentees together.

Enter my business associate and friend, organizational psychologist Dr. Harvey Thomas. Harvey had been one of those invaluable resources shared by Ewing Kauffman, and he had done good work for Mr. Kauffman's organization and Helzberg Diamonds. He knew business, but more important, he knew intimately how human dynamics work. I would regularly meet for breakfast with Harvey to throw out ideas, and he would help polish them into better, more structured ones.

My first step was a "fishing expedition" to the Kansas City business leaders I had known through the years. I picked those with a bent for service—after all, we wouldn't be paying them—and those who didn't seem consumed by ego. There's nothing wrong with ego, but our focus would be on serving Mentees, so a need to always be the show's star would stand in the way of that help.

Walt Rychlewski, Bill Eddy, and Bill Reisler laughing at the HEMP's first meeting.

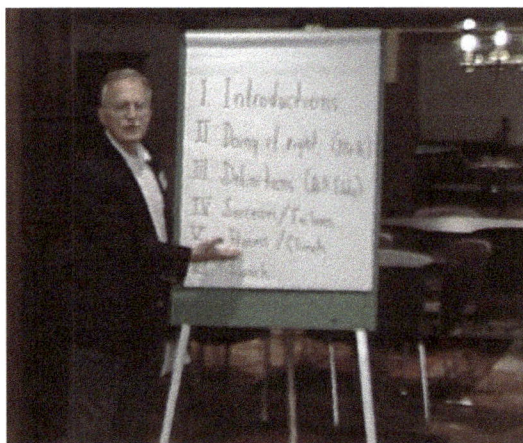

Harvey Thomas setting the agenda for the first meeting that will help form HEMP.

Also, I secured sponsorship from the Entrepreneurial Council at the University of Missouri–Kansas City. My friend from UMKC, Bill Eddy, had been instrumental in the "I'm going to do this!" decision. The council's name, along with the Ewing Marion Kauffman Foundation's sponsorship, lent gravitas to the fledgling idea and made marketing sense. The people I wanted to approach had more invitations to volunteer than they could accept in a decade, so I figured any edge I could add would be helpful.

The simple invitation letter said the following:

> I am writing to a small group of entrepreneurs about a new program sponsored by UMKC's Entrepreneurial Council and the Ewing Marion Kauffman Foundation that will help budding Kansas City–area entrepreneurs develop their businesses.
>
> I am in need of mentors despite being raised in a family where business was dinner-table conversation!
>
> Upon thanking one of my greatest mentors, Ewing Kauffman, he said, "That's okay. You will help somebody someday."
>
> Most entrepreneurs have had at least one great mentor! Maybe for one of these entrepreneurs, that could be you!
>
> If you would enjoy helping an enterprising entrepreneur, please fill out the enclosed form and mail it back to me by March 17, 1995. I look forward to hearing from you!
>
> Sincerely,
> Barnett C. Helzberg, Jr.

And, yes, instead of ending with a paragraph of flattery about why this new venture would be so lucky to acquire the recipient's considerable talent and visibility, I attached an application. It asked why these leaders were interested in mentoring and what skills they brought and then ended with a request for a resume! Looking back, I shake my head a little at this final requirement. I was writing to people who likely hadn't applied for anything in thirty years. Little did I know, this would set a precedent for our future.

My dad always said, "It's fine to learn from your mistakes. It's better to learn from others' mistakes." Between my decisive moment in the mirror and sending this letter, Harvey and I had been digging into mentoring articles from business experts to understand what mattered and to avoid their mistakes. From that investigation, we added to the Mentor invitation letter a two-page outline of what we intended to do and a general sketch of how we would go about it. I even boldly created a tagline I thought we might use to market the program to Mentees. It read, "Ask the One Who Has Done It . . . Your Access to Wisdom, Experience, and Battle Scars!"

> **" It's fine to learn from your mistakes. It's better to learn from others' mistakes. "**

The Initial Structure

Here is the HEMP setup proposal, along with some thinking behind the program's principles.

Mentoring Program Proposal

The purpose of this mentoring program is to bring successful, established Kansas City–area businesspeople together with business owners who believe they can benefit from the opportunity to develop a one-on-one relationship with a knowledgeable, experienced individual. The ultimate goal will be to enhance business growth and success.

[A love for Kansas City drove much of HEMP's creation. Our contributions would center on Kansas City's growing success.]

> **A Mentor can listen, help talk out issues, and even offer suggestions and options for consideration in a nonbinding and supportive fashion. The establishment of this program can serve as an avenue to bring special assistance to individuals who otherwise might not be able to match up with an experienced and successful individual.**

[We were determined there would be no expectation of an expert giving definitive answers to problems! Instead of acting as consultants, the Mentors were going to be a sounding board to help Mentees bring out the answers they already know.]

The typical Mentor will be a successful professional with proven business skills and knowledge who has an interest in helping others. Each will be recruited individually by a leader of the program. Hopefully, this will avoid including someone who is not an ideal Mentor.

[It did occur to me how embarrassing it is to apply for a job and get turned down. Ouch! Over the years, we evolved ways to handle this issue differently and, I think, better. You'll see how this process changed in the years ahead by recommending alternate programs, or as we call it, no cold turndowns.]

66 No cold turndowns. 99

1 Mentor and Mentee meetings can range from one session to a long-term relationship. The team involved will decide this by its actions, not officially.

[We later got more structured about this issue and many others. But at the start, you can see we

were concerned about too many rules—too much "You should . . ." and "You must . . ."—killing the focus on what I saw as the key element of mentoring success: the chemistry of the relationship.]

2   Program leaders will suggest matchups of Mentor-Mentee teams based on the biographies of the individuals involved. The Mentor will emphasize her or his areas of greatest strength in the biography, and the prospective Mentee will highlight her or his most significant areas of need. Ideally, the Mentee will have the opportunity to visit three potential Mentors. If the chemistry is workable, there is no reason the Mentee cannot enjoy contact with more than one Mentor.

[Although we didn't spell it out, I was already sure that Mentors and Mentees shouldn't be in the same industry. Mr. Kauffman taught me how much insight it's possible to gain about your business if your resources come from outside it. What mattered more than similar industries were our chemistry and parallel challenges.]

3   Our job will be to facilitate and encourage these personal relationships to happen, not to create or make them. These Mentors are deposits rich in knowledge, and we will provide a map to this wonderful bank of knowledge.

[How do you orchestrate two people falling in love? Matchmakers try to offer best-chance wisdom, but they have no power to infuse that "she's the one" feeling that gives openness and joy. So, we would set up the potential matches as best we could and see what happened from there.]

4   Because there are personal relationships involved, there must be an easy way out for both parties. The Mentees initiate the meetings, so by doing nothing further, the program is terminated from the Mentee side. Perhaps the Mentor's lack of availability will end it for her or his part. The Mentee need not worry that he has offended someone in the community. These relationships can go from one visit to many and might take place very few times in a year. Mentors must be able to bow out gracefully if they feel their time is abused or feel they cannot help the individual.

[We would later label this process "no-fault divorce." It seemed clear from the start that Neil Sedaka's 1960s hit "Breaking Up Is Hard to Do" would always hold true. Maybe caring entrepreneurs would enter the experience more readily if they knew there was a way out that would not incur an exorbitant relational price to haunt them.]

5   We must be careful not to document or track the results in any formal way. It must not become burdensome, embarrassing, or a hassle. My own experience of years with Mr. K would not have happened if we had to do paperwork.

[In time, others would show us ways to add unoppressive accountability, but my squeamishness about lists to check and forms to fill out was evident from the start.]

6 The responsibility for initiating a visit rests with the Mentee, who calls and says, "I'd like your advice!" It all starts there.

[This was intended to take the pressure off the Mentors who already had more than enough to do and didn't need one more obligation. We figured in time a natural communication flow between the two would develop but starting with responsibility on the one seeking help seemed to make sense.]

7 Mentees will be encouraged to get advice from two or more individuals. These loose relationships can be beneficial even in the case of widely spaced meetings or phone visits. It reminds the Mentee that there can be multiple answers to the same question and enables the Mentee to seek out the specialized genius resident in an individual.

[We figured smart entrepreneurs would be doing this anyway—seeking advice from more than one source. Formalizing the idea might eliminate a propensity to hide the fact that Mentees were asking others. It might also give Mentors freedom from feeling the need to be a one-stop shop for everything.]

8 Potential Mentors will be sought from a variety of communities, with a particular focus on minorities and women to ensure we represent our city as a whole. There will be no effort to match up Mentors and Mentees by race or gender, however. The only criterion for pairing individuals will be the right skills.

[This effort—diversity—mattered to us from the start. Accomplishing it the way we would have liked has always been a challenge and one we are continuing to realize twenty-five years later.]

9 Both the Mentee and Mentor will sign an agreement recognizing that whoever takes bad advice made the error! This would be a hold harmless agreement and would also make a point to the Mentees.

[The Mentors might raise questions about what kind of liability they could be assuming. Even at our first organizational meeting, someone suggested that we not use the term clients because it might suggest we would be acting as consultants. That question needed to be off the table quickly, thus this clause that absolves both parties of legal liability.]

10 We will stay away from any approach that asks participants to spend any specified times together. Relationships will grow or not grow naturally. Screening for Mentors and Mentees will be a judgment call. We will look forward to success stories, recognizing that the glass will be half full if we can help some of our Mentees. We realize that a washout rate is inherent in this type of program. Testimonials will tell the story.

["Failure is not an option" would never be a mantra for us because that's not how entrepreneurs work. There is no perfect person or idea or business approach. Some of the best learning and strategies in business come from decisions that tanked. We drew from Thomas Edison's example: it took thousands of experiments to create the electric light bulb. HEMP would grow like that, too. We would win some and lose some and admitting that right up front would free us to keep focused on learning better ways.

Also, we initially said we would not ask participants to spend specified times together. Our expectation on this would change in the years ahead.]

11 We will offer this program to the KC Entrepreneurs Club and other local organizations where ambitious people congregate. Mentees can be recruited through the Chambers of Commerce in the Kansas City area, such as the Kansas City Chamber, Black Chamber, Hispanic Chamber, and other like institutions.

[This plan sounded good on paper, but in reality, marketing attempts turned more to a lot of looking here and there with people inviting others they knew. This unstructured approach was enough to get going, and getting going was the goal.

In time, this marketing challenge would mostly take care of itself, thanks to word of mouth. A participant tells a golfing buddy how much he's enjoying the program. Someone else hears of us the way one Mentee did when his bankers suggested he join HEMP.]

12 We recognize that most mentoring programs have been failures—too formal, too structured, and not reflective of the personal nature of the relationships sought. We will zealously guard against this taking place, including asking Mentors and Mentees how to improve the program.

[Voicing this reality clearly might help some to know we had thought of the possibility of failure already and had a plan: feedback. We might not get it right at first, but if you will tell us where we are off, we'll hear you and adjust.]

13 This program will start in a small way, so our mistakes at start-up will not be magnified. After phase one, it can be grown.

[A long time ago someone shared this African proverb: "If you are going to test the depth of the water, don't jump into the water with both feet." That seemed smart—one foot in and you might still recover to test another day; both feet in and drowning is always a possibility. We didn't want the big business players we sought as Mentors to dismiss this venture because we were starting small. But we also had no intention of waiting around until we had planned an impressive mentoring behemoth. No, get on with it. Learn as you go. Fail small, succeed big.]

We had extended the invitation. Now we needed Mentors to respond.

HEMP's first meeting in the lower level/basement of the Helzberg home.

CHAPTER 3

From Passion to Pilot

n response to the invitation, fifteen business leaders agreed to meet in our basement—the lower level as Shirley calls it and still reminds me—on a morning in early May, committing three hours to talk about this mentoring venture. As Shirley and I prepared to host, we realized we were short on having enough coffee for the large urn we usually used for big gatherings. Shirley gathered several bags of various coffee samples, and we dumped them all together to make a brew that tasted . . . surprisingly good!

Harvey Thomas agreed to facilitate the meeting. We planned to open with Bill Eddy giving a little talk on what mentoring was. He would explain that the word *mentor* comes from a character in Homer's *Odyssey* named Mentor who nurtured and taught a young

Dr. Harvey Thomas

man all he knew about leading. Then Bill would apply that picture of mentoring to the idea we were proposing. After Bill, I would be interviewed about my experience with Ewing Kauffman as a mentor. To get folks involved and talking, we would go around and ask the attendees about their own experiences working with a mentor, what worked and what didn't. We would collect the takeaways on a flip chart.

Then we would go right on to the meat of the meeting—to brainstorming the structure, policies, and marketing for the program. Business thinkers thinking business.

It didn't work out completely according to plan, and what a gift!

The fault and credit go to a Kansas City real estate magnate named Barney Karbank. Barney had been stunningly successful in the commercial real estate arena and was known and admired by nearly every success-focused business leader in the city. Because of his stature, most of us expected to hear a gracious story crediting someone who contributed to his success, and that would be it. Box checked; assignment completed to help bring credibility to the power of mentoring supported by the guy everyone wanted to be.

But Barney didn't use this platform to slide over the surface; he opened his heart to us.

He told us about a two-year-old boy contracting polio and the struggle during his next eight years when, bound by large, bulky braces on two-thirds of his body, he tried unsuccessfully to keep up with the other kids. He spoke about a father who owned a fish market but wanted something better for his boy and pushed him toward real estate. These were the customers at his fish market who seemed to drive the nicest cars and wear the most expensive suits. He went on with stories of business mentors who taught so much but sometimes with the scariest of tactics, like assigning him the toughest accounts and pushing him out the door. When there were turning-point successes, he credited lucky breaks, but mistakes were his alone.

To have Barney Karbank lead out like this rewired the room.

Each business leader who followed him moved immediately into his or her version of an unvarnished "how I got here" story. A woman in the group talked about how discouraging it was to try to get financing when she began because of the prevailing attitude that women couldn't run a successful business. The owner of a very successful restaurant described how as a young man he had been turned away from a popular burger place because he was Mexican. That rejection was one of many, but he decided to let it motivate him and went after education, military service, and American citizenship. There was laughter and muffled cheers when he related that after building a successful restaurant, he was able to buy the building that housed that burger place.

It's hard to describe the emotion many expressed while revealing their most difficult business times and what it had meant that a more experienced leader had walked beside them through it. I don't have enough knowledge in understanding people to say how this all unleashed, but I know this: it was magic. Harvey and I had planned for a break halfway through the meeting, but he wisely said nothing and allowed it to flow. When an experience like that is happening, you would be a fool to pause it for anything, and Harvey was anything but a fool.

When we finished, fourteen of the fifteen who attended said they were interested in being Mentors. We went on to brainstorm the next steps. Business leaders that we were, we headed straight to the bottom line:

- We needed some training so the mentoring we are delivering is top-notch.
- We needed to get people who want mentoring and are mentorable.

We quickly put together a time to meet for a training session Harvey Thomas offered to create. And we decided we would scout for Mentees by going after people we knew already.

We had crossed into uncharted but compelling territory when one of the participants said, "We're talking mentoring here. But it seems to me what we are selling is friendships.

Barnett C. Helzberg, Jr. pitching his idea for HEMP.

A group of Kansas City's top business minds gather to brainstorm what would become HEMP.

They're just friendships between very experienced business folks and those who want to grow." Others nodded their agreement.

He got it. We got it.

I have looked back many times and wondered how strongly and quickly HEMP would have become the open, relationship-rich organization our participants now tell us we are if Barney had not made the choice to open up the way he did. I'll always be grateful, both for the organization's sake and for the sake of the hundreds of Mentees in the future, that HEMP had this jump start in becoming a place where it was safe to say, "I need help," and find stellar-quality support and assistance rather than judgment and shame.

Now, with a heart and a couple of simple next steps established for the organization, all we needed to be open for business was *everything else*.

Business leaders sharing stories at HEMP's first meeting.

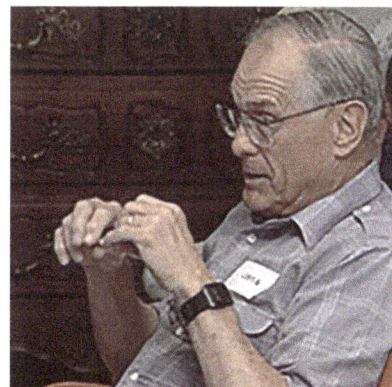

Chuck Hoffman giving his two cents about the program.

HELZBERG ENTREPRENEURIAL MENTORING PROGRAM

The Shirley and Barnett C.
Helzberg, Jr. Foundation
4520 Main, Suite 1050
Kansas City, MO 64111-1816
(816) 753-7776 phone
(816) 753-8776 fax

Founding Mentors
Henry W. Bloch
Joe Brandmeyer
Eileen Cohen
Charles Delgado
Cheryl Womack Elliott
Bob Epsten
Chuck Hoffman
Barney Karbank
Manny Lopez
Mel Mallin
Alex Masson
Harry McCray
Frank Oddo
John Palmer
Bill Reisler
Jim Roath
Bob Rogers
Bob Shapiro

Steering Committee
Bill Eddy
Barnett C. Helzberg, Jr.
Kurt Mueller
Walt Rychlewski
Robert J. Sherwood
Michie Slaughter
Ray Smilor
Harvey Thomas

Co-sponsored by
UMKC Bloch School Council for Entrepreneurial and
Center for Entrepreneurial Leadership, Inc., Ewing Marion Kauffman Foundation

In photograph above: Henry W. Bloch, Danny O'Neill, Barnett C. Helzberg, Jr., and Rick Krska.

Getting Mentees and Creating Mentor Training

In the months from June to September, we focused on setup. We had left that basement with commitments from a troop of magnificent businesspeople. But we had yet to clarify what the experience would look like, what mentees we would target and recruit, a way to match mentees to mentors, and just enough structure to make a pilot program work.

To get there, we created a roughed-out description of what we would be selling in our search for Mentees. Right away we decided *selling* was the wrong term, however, as the program would be free to Mentees. So *selling* became *offering*.

One significant advantage of our program was the endorsement and participation of Henry Bloch, one of the cofounders of the H&R Block tax and investment mega-enterprise. Henry's star power gave credibility, and we played it up by listing our Mentors on our HEMP letterhead. It worked out perfectly because his name was first alphabetically. (I'd love to leave you with the impression that this mentoring idea so dazzled one of Kansas City's most prominent business players that he signed on at once. In reality, Henry was married to my beautiful first cousin, so he may have been thinking how awkward family gatherings might be if he said no. At any rate, his presence gave us the boost of attention and credibility that helped the launch. You play the cards in your hand, and I was lucky enough to be holding a card with Henry Bloch's name on it.)

In follow-up meetings, we came up with some good-enough expectations of what a Mentor would do and what characteristics might make someone a good Mentee. We also created what we called a Steering Committee, tasked with screening candidates and then matching them with Mentors. Informally, we described the committee members as *marriage brokers*. That was likely as useful a description as any.

Since we had a good pool of Mentors, we exercised our options to match each Mentee with three Mentors. Finding relationship chemistry was enough of a blindfolded dartboard exercise that we would do well to give options and see what happened. Mentees could utilize all three, just one, or some more than others. When Mentees asked how long they were committing to participate, we dodged the question because we didn't have a clue. We gave answers like it would depend on how the relationships developed or other equally vague responses. This was a pilot after all. It was better not to commit to definitive answers with long-term consequences if we didn't know.

The Mentee candidate acquisition process centered mostly on the Mentors talking to newer businesspeople they thought might be interested. We were looking for people who showed humility and the ability to listen and who seemed to have that spark of success already in them.

For instance, I first noticed Danny O'Neill, who would become an early Mentee, at a New Year's Eve event sponsored by the Kansas City Symphony. I would later learn his fledgling coffee business had no advertising money. To pump up attention, he offered to supply and personally serve coffee for various charity events.

Danny tells the story of a guy coming up to the coffee bar that New Year's Eve announcing, "I've had my eyes on you! We are starting a mentoring program for entrepreneurs. Would you be interested?" Danny responded, "I've had my eyes on you, too. That's your third cup of decaf." Despite my overindulgence, we connected and agreed to meet.

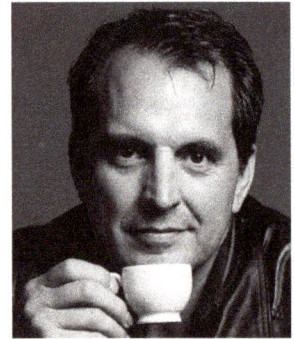

Danny O'Neill

A few months later, we talked about HEMP. It turned out the timing was perfect because Danny was desperate for help. He recalls, "In college, I majored in international studies, not business, so when I started the company in 1993, I knew almost nothing about running it. By the time I met Barnett, I was working seventeen to twenty-one hours a day, seven days a week and was completely exhausted. So when Barnett invited me to talk about whether or not I needed business mentoring, it wasn't simply 'yes.' I proceeded to vomit a ton of problems I was facing." This kind of transparency was what we were seeking in Mentees and Mentors.

What we were offering seemed to make sense to him and others. We would provide at no cost a trusting relationship with an experienced, vetted advisor who had no personal agenda other than the best interests of the Mentee. Consultants, lawyers, bankers, and other paid experts get money for their services, which inserts a level of potential conflict of interest. Not so with HEMP Mentors. Their work would have no success measure but the success of their Mentee.

By late August, we had gathered fourteen Mentee candidates to interview. In light of how sophisticated the Mentee application and screening process would become in the years ahead, we smile now at the simple questions we decided to ask these potential participants—rudimentary but good enough.

- Who has been your best advisor up to now? What made that person helpful?
- How do you happen to be in this business?
- You wake up at 4:00 a.m. Share the content of your mind.
- What decision you made in the last eighteen months was most correct?
- What decision would you make differently?
- What do you see happening down the road? Any sticky wickets you must negotiate?

Deciding Focus

During this setup flurry, we happened onto a piece of advice that would turn out to be one of our most significant foundational decisions.

At a UMKC meeting, I was sitting next to Kurt Mueller, who was director of Entrepreneurial Services at accounting firm Ernst & Young and later headed entrepreneurial activities for the Kauffman Foundation. When I told him about the idea for this program, he said immediately, "You don't want to do start-ups."

This advice was a dramatic moment for me. I said, "Oh my gosh! You are right." I didn't start Helzberg Diamonds, and the mentors had led companies for such a long time that their help would be most useful to those who were past the start-up stage. We would be wasting remarkable resources if we didn't look for Mentees who were further along.

The smartest decision we made as we started? To focus on second-stage entrepreneurs.

At this decision, Mel Mallin, a Kansas City pioneer in the conversion of classic buildings to lofts, decided not to participate. He explained, "You are going to pick only the people who are going to make it."

He had a point, and I knew it. The story came to my mind of my friend Bob. While awaiting a heart procedure, he was assured by the nurse, "No need to worry. You're going to be fine." "How can you be so sure?" he asked nervously. "Oh, it's your doctor," she smiled. "He only takes the ones who are going to make it."

But we weren't deterred. We were committed to this venture to help individuals and to ensure the future economic stability and prosperity of Kansas City. The city would need to see successful small businesses not just endure but become more successful. These second-stage people had the best chance of helping with that challenge. To do that, they would likely need mentoring because as some say, "What got you where you are won't necessarily get you where you want to go." Mentors could provide questions and expertise to help these successful second-stage folks keep growing.

A tactical consideration was an influence, too. We had to prove this mentoring idea was viable. If all the Mentees we had taken on went out of business, there would be no future for HEMP.

> ❝ **Fail small, succeed big.** ❞

The second smartest decision we made in these early days? To keep the pilot small. Remember, as noted earlier, it is better to fail small and succeed big. We had all been in business long enough to still carry the scars from ignoring that wisdom. We settled on inviting only six Mentees to the pilot.

And the third smartest decision? To keep the structure simple. Bill Eddy from UMKC knew me well enough to know administration was my great weakness and insisted we have help to keep the logistics running smoothly. He pointed us to Joe Rog, a UMKC intern studying business administration. Joe came on board to help as administrative coordinator and quickly became an enormous asset to the organization. He was the right man at the right time.

Bill Eddy

Harvey Thomas put together a "Mentor training session" that ended with an agreement that we would meet quarterly to evaluate and keep learning together. Fortunately, Harvey was a master at crafting questions that led people to discover and articulate the answers themselves (a skill we would later push and push and push with Mentors). In this training session, it was the Mentors who wound up describing what they would do. When the time ended, their instructions for themselves boiled down to these:

- The structure of mentoring is loose.
- Mentees initiate meetings with Mentors.
- The length of each relationship and the frequency of its meetings are flexible.
- Relationship forming is the highest priority.
- To keep perspectives fresh, no Mentor-Mentee matches will be from the same industry.

Mentor, Ray Pitman, with all his Mentees he lovingly called "Ray's Kids."

With these loosely knit processes and expectations, Mentees and Mentors were named, matched, and invited to a launch meeting for introductions and messy but optimistic expectations of what everyone had signed on to accomplish.

Someplace in all this, we decided we needed to name the organization. I wanted to name it after Mr. Kauffman in appreciation for all he had done for me. But the others involved took a vote and overruled me. That's how it became the Helzberg Entrepreneurial Mentoring Program. Someone pointed out that the acronym for our top-flight business program was HEMP—an illegal substance at the time—so any reservations on my part vanished. What fun we could have with that one!

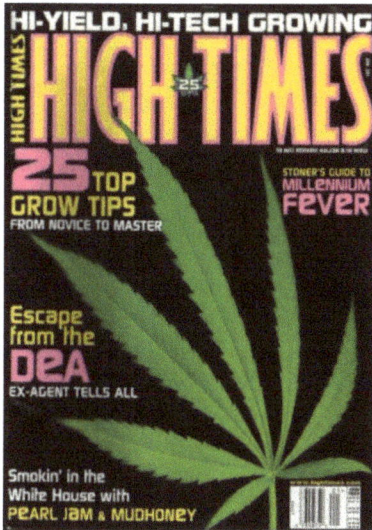

Our name has continued to be a source of fun through the years. For example, when a new president started his or her term with our program, I had a subscription to *High Times*, an American monthly magazine founded in 1974 about marijuana, anonymously sent to the president's home. And then there was the time Christina Dreiling, Chuck Hoffman, Ray Pitman, and I were having lunch at Houlihan's restaurant. I was wearing a shirt with our HEMP logo, and the young server commented on it. I proceeded to explain that I was in the marijuana business, and the young man and I had a colorful conversation about what I described as a small West Coast distributorship. I asked him if he wanted to come to my car. He replied, "I'm on the clock, but maybe I could after work?" My comrades played along, and we all had a good laugh together. Keep HEMP Fun!

With that, we launched the pilot and were off and running. It was a start, and as any entrepreneur will tell you, in the beginning, movement is all you need.

The "HEMPtations" performing at Celebrate HEMP in 2005.

Cynthia Savage, Missy Love, and Renee McDougal peek out the window at Celebrate HEMP.

Mike Pandzik, Henry Wash, Gordon Harton, Margaret Reynolds, and Dan Stalp unwind at a cocktail hour.

Part 3: Organizing & Reorganizing

(1996–2010)

Retreat keynote speaker John Mackey, Whole Foods Market CEO and co-founder.

CHAPTER 4

Learning By Doing

In late 1995, the pilot was underway with a manageable six Mentees and a Mentor pool of twenty-six available to help them. The size worked well because, as my friend Jon Davies used to say, "I'd rather own a small gold mine than a large silver mine." These Mentor-Mentee pairs looked like gold to us.

> ❝ I'd rather own a small gold mine than a large silver mine. ❞

Mentees were from a mixed bag of businesses: a coffee roaster, an organizing store, a restaurant, a technology entity, and a marketing enterprise, etc. We made introductions and the one-on-one mentoring sessions began.

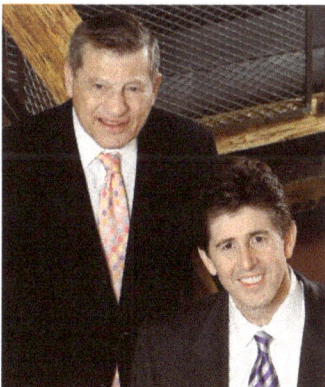

Barnett C. Helzberg, Jr. with his first Mentee, Rick Krska.

One of my early Mentees was Rick Krska, who had started a laser cartridge recycling facility. When Rick came to HEMP, he had fifty-seven employees and $10 million in sales. His primary concern was fear of growing too fast. Prior to HEMP, Rick was doing FastTrac (an early stage entrepreneurial program sponsored by the Kauffman Foundation), and I wrote Rick to see if he would be interested in our program. According to Rick, "I was flattered to get a letter from Barnett Helzberg. I called the number on the letter and was surprised when Barnett personally answered the phone."

Bill Eddy and I met with Rick, and he seemed almost too good to be true. Before we accepted Rick into our program, however, I had to visit Rick's facility to "smell him out" and make sure his business and story were as solid of a fit for HEMP as it seemed from our conversation. I toured his business and was even more impressed. We continued the conversation from a morning at his worksite to a lunch at Mr. Goodcents because they had free drink refills. (I love a good deal!)

At that meeting, Rick said to me, "If you're going to be my Mentor, you have to come to North Carolina to meet my biggest supplier." Okay, then! We got on a plane and headed southeast. The supplier gave me a shirt, which I was very thankful for and wore each time I visited Rick's office. That tradition has grown, and I continue to enjoy wearing shirts or hats connected to

Barnett C. Helzberg, Jr. wearing his "mensch" socks from notes to self, llc at a meeting.

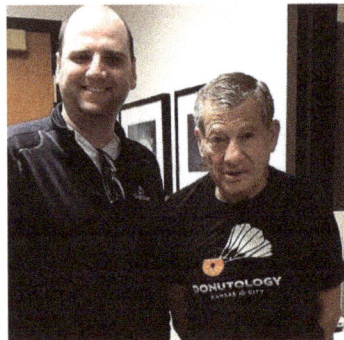

Andrew Cameron smiles while his Mentor, Barnett C. Helzberg, Jr., reps his company, Donutology.

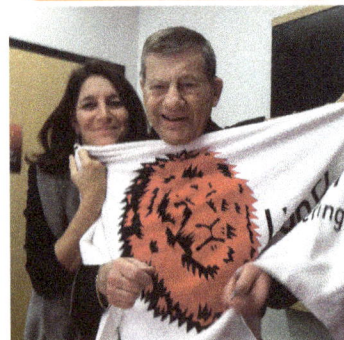

Laura Lee Jones snuggling Barnett C. Helzberg, Jr. in her LionShare, Inc. flag.

our HEMPers, especially when I meet with them. Rick is now a Mentor and his business continues to grow and evolve. In a newspaper interview about the mentoring experience, he told a reporter, "Initially there can be a certain 'uptightness' about dealing with each other. The Mentors don't want to interfere, and the Mentees don't want to be pests. But you must get past that. If you can relax into the relationship, it will probably turn out to be a great thing for both of you." I didn't feel uptight at all, which is why we have to keep getting feedback from Mentees! Relax we did, and he was right: it was great for us both.

Because the Mentor group had agreed to meet quarterly to evaluate and share learning, we started adjusting the initial setup decisions almost immediately. Keep this, get rid of that—that's how it works when good thinkers are creating together. These enthusiastic businesspeople raised questions and helped one another find answers while working together to generate resources for their Mentees. We were cocreating our unique version of a resource that had helped us, and the energy was palpable.

By 1999, a survey by the Kauffman Foundation that interviewed Mentees who had completed the program found that 100 percent of them would recommend HEMP to other entrepreneurs. In addition, 71 percent who had experienced a growth in sales and 67 percent who had experienced a growth in the number of employees attributed some of this increase to HEMP.

Between that simple 1995 beginning and the 1999 measures of success, we had been tweaking the program. Our experiences as Mentors drove some of the changes; Mentees pushed others as we asked them what needed to change. Some were relatively simple. For example, we had set up the relationships so only Mentees took the initiative to connect. But some didn't do so because the prestige of their Mentor intimidated them. They would think, "Gosh, if I called her, would she have a clue as to who I am?" The Mentors shared enough innate humility that this caveat hadn't occurred to any of them. But softening this rule was an easy change. Others came with more complexity—and sometimes some more-than-rowdy discussion!

We thought about making changes the way a university we had heard about designed their system of sidewalks. When they put up new buildings, sidewalks didn't go in immediately. They would wait to see where students naturally walked, then turn those beaten paths into something more permanent. This seemed to make good sense: see what HEMPers were asking about, or how they used or didn't use the help we envisioned, and let those factors tell us where to change.

Cleaning Up Expectations

Settling on the Program Length

Remember how fluid we were in answering questions about how long the mentoring would last? We chose this route to emphasize that this mentoring experience was more about building a trust-based relationship than about completing a program.

But a hitch appeared we hadn't considered, our number of Mentees were increasing each year.

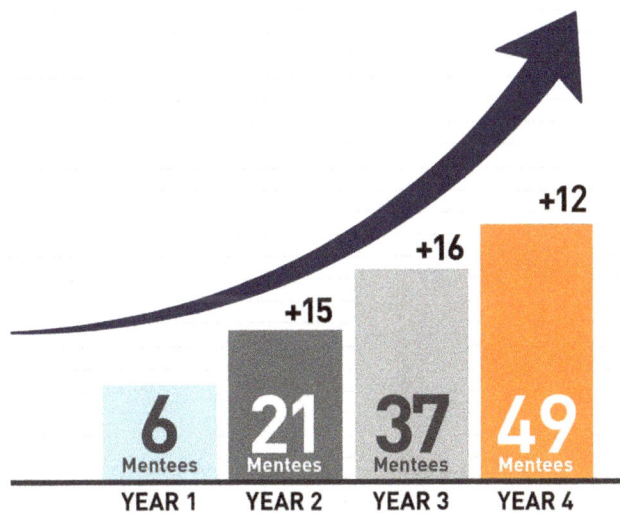

	+15	+16	+12
6 Mentees	21 Mentees	37 Mentees	49 Mentees
YEAR 1	YEAR 2	YEAR 3	YEAR 4

By the time we reached 1999, *none of the original six Mentees had left his or her mentoring relationships*, and the Steering Committee was getting a little nervous. We had thirty-eight Mentors and forty-nine Mentees, nearly one hundred participants. In a planning meeting, someone asked nervously, "Have we hit critical mass? Should we limit terms?"

When surveyed on this question, Mentees responded with an "all-caps "NO!" That was fine for a duo like Mr. K and me, but what would these long-term involvements do to an organization?

Were we headed toward becoming one of those snooty social clubs with a significant participant list but only a handful doing the work and only another handful profiting from first-class help?

However, the problem we were solving was a healthy one: entrepreneurs came for help, received help, and then didn't want to leave! Wrestling with this dilemma produced a solution. Maybe we could say the mentoring term was two years (soon to be adjusted to three years). During that time, our office would facilitate Mentor-Mentee connections. After that, the relationships could continue, but we wouldn't be tending to them officially. It has been gratifying to see some of these relationships have continued for years.

Defining program length also raised a suggestion that we designate the group starting its two-year experience together as a class, such as the Class of 1996. Maybe this would help Mentees feel a measure of group identity that went beyond the relationship with their Mentors. As it would turn out, emphasis on the class relationships would become one of HEMP's best resources to develop long-term connections that lasted far beyond Mentees' graduations.

Also, we decided to offer a new designation: Senior Mentee. Once participants were finished mentoring, they could become a Senior Mentee and would be asked to pay a yearly fee in return for invitations to all programs, events, and publication subscriptions. They were welcome to continue formal or informal relationships, and making new ones was completely open.

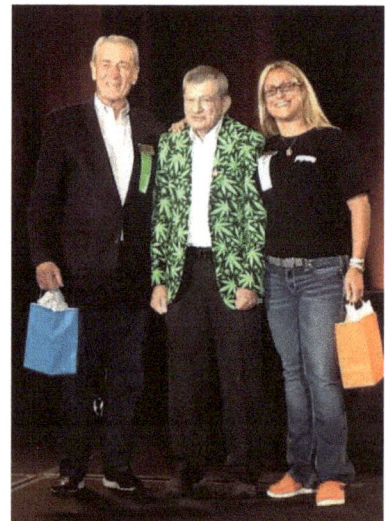

Jack Schmid and Barnett C. Helzberg, Jr., celebrate Brandy McCombs' graduation from HEMP.

At the time, we were unknowingly laying the foundation for what would become very powerful HEMP resources: the alumni, Mentee graduates who completed our three-year program. We now call those Senior Mentees our Fellows.

Establishing the Definition of Second-Stage Entrepreneurs

Once we got off the ground and more Mentees signed on, we began to realize that "an entrepreneur leading a business in second-stage development" meant different things to different people. This definition is no Webster's dictionary thing. In the spirit of fairness, we would need to align our thinking more closely with our wording. When Mentees are "ultimate decision-makers" for companies of similar size and revenue, they would be talking the same language and facing many of the same problems. Such similarities would help draw them together naturally.

In a conversation that the meeting recorder described coyly as "a monstrous argument," the Steering Committee decided on setting revenue and employee expectations. They started with $1 million or more in annual revenue and a minimum of ten to twenty employees as our working definition of "second stage." These numbers would slide about as we tried them. In time, we adjusted employee numbers to account for tech and other firms that had few employees but substantial revenue.

Attendance Requirements

Shortly after HEMP began, we required active participants to have four one-on-one meetings with their Mentors and to attend four events per year.

Laird Goldsborough and Joanne Montgomery lead a HEMP event on social entrepreneurism in Barnett's Basement.

Attendance requirements for this "don't fence me in" entrepreneurial crowd? Yes, but for different reasons than you might be thinking. Some of the Mentees told us how tough it was to pull themselves away from the office to meet with their Mentor or to attend an event—even if they knew they would profit! Basically, these work-obsessed, mostly out-of-balance business entrepreneurs need a kick in the pants to take a break. It didn't take long for the Mentors to recall their business-building years and agree. This is a challenge we continue to stress to all our Mentees: you need to take time to work on your business, not in it.

This requirement quickly showed itself to be a service rather than a duty.

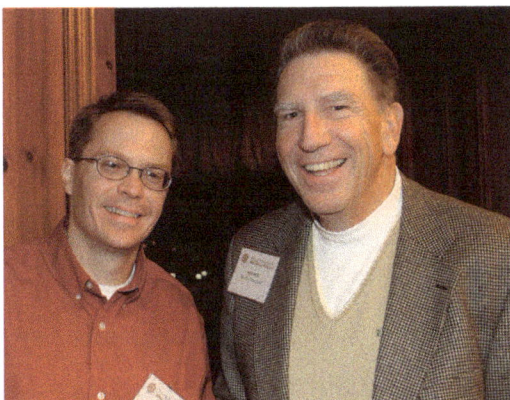

Jim Fitts and Michie Slaughter pose for a picture at the 2004 HEMP retreat.

Pay to Play

I'll admit it. This was a tough one. From the beginning, I had imagined the service to be free to Mentees. But as each year passed, more HEMPers spoke up about reasons participation fees could help the program. I wasn't sure, but I kept listening. "We all put more value on something we pay for," they argued. "The income might help our bottom line," others said. But most persuasively, I finally heard, "Maybe it serves everyone. If people pay something, it may help sort out some of those who were just dabbling and never intended to commit to the learning that makes mentoring worth it. This could be an easy way to quietly ensure that Mentees mean business and Mentors aren't wasting their valuable gift of time."

We had convinced one another and adjusted the policy. The approach was an interesting one. When we began a participation fee in 1999, we asked for $100 the first year, $750 the second, and $1,000 the third. We reasoned that the value of what Mentees were receiving would only increase the longer they participated. However, we quickly found charging the same fee each year was preferred, so we charged $1,000 per year.

> **We would adjust this participation fee slowly over time using the "Boil the Rat" philosophy captured in a fable describing a rat being slowly boiled alive. (Technically, the fable features a frog, but we liked the idea of the demise of an ugly rat more than a cute frog.) The premise is this: If a rat is suddenly put into boiling water, it will jump out. But if the rat is put into tepid water brought to a boil slowly, it will not perceive the danger.**

We have adjusted our fee marginally several times over the years. At this writing, it is $6,000 per year. Our goal is twofold: to keep the cost modest and affordable and to support HEMPers by creating a sustainable organization whose value continues to grow.

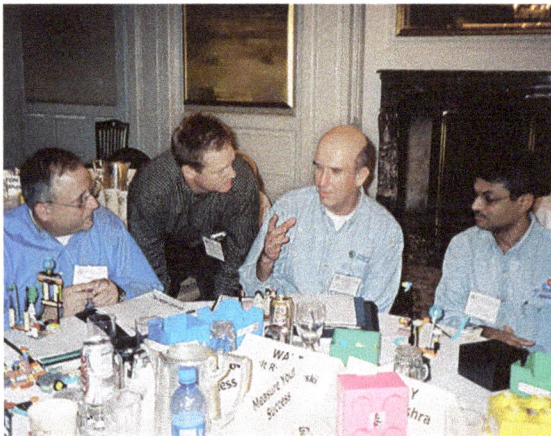

Eric Morgenstern, Ed Nelson, Walt Rychlewski, and Sanjay Mishra work together on a team building exercise.

Janene Ervin, Elizabeth Amirahmadi, Jim Stuelke, and Bob Shapiro grab a glass of wine at a HEMP event.

Supporting the Matches

Multiple Mentors?

We launched HEMP with the ambitious plan of offering each Mentee three potential Mentors. After getting to know all three, he or she could choose one or reach out to more than one for individual needs. In retrospect, we were quite generous to say the least!

Initially, there was a method to what would develop into mini madness. Our thinking was this: Relationships are everything. We have no backup plan. Connections can't be assigned or forced; chemistry grows, or it doesn't. So how might we best offer Mentees the potential for relational chemistry? Our best guess was this multiple-Mentors idea.

However, we quickly came to hear from Mentees that the number of Mentors often intimidated them. Out of sheer practical time considerations, they didn't pursue all of the Mentors, causing excellent resources to sit idle.

Belinda Waggoner meets with her Mentor, Jack Schmid.

We also hadn't counted on the administrative complexity of organizing and supporting these multiple and sometimes fluid matches. It became overwhelming to keep up with who was meeting with whom and when and how the matches were working.

Fortunately, there was a reason these initial years were considered an extended pilot, and this part of the pilot taught us we had made the wrong choice. Going forward, the Mentor-Mentee matches became focused on creating a robust one-to-one connection with multiple Mentors as the exception rather than the rule.

Facilitating the Matches

When we talked about relationships being "facilitated," we found from feedback that Mentees wanted more than just initial matching from us. They sought check-ins from our office to see how the connection was going. "Don't be so scared of hurting people's feelings," they told us. "Check up on us!"

To an organization whose initial charter leaned overwhelmingly in the direction of descriptors like "loose" and "unstructured," we hesitated. Early on, we had been telling participants that Mentees could drop out of the program by just not calling their Mentor anymore. Mentors could withdraw from their Mentees by simply claiming an overloaded schedule. We weren't sophisticated in how to address this issue, as demonstrated by this awkward attempt.

Finally, someone pointed out these mentoring relationships were delicate and needed careful maintenance. Perhaps they were like a garden: no tending and weeds could take over. We agreed that we were about relationships, but that not all happen automatically. Ones that don't are wasting everyone's time. Mentors are a renewable, nonpolluting, cost-free, priceless resource and deserve to be used effectively.

We became more proactive in checking for the weeds. We had our office administrator make periodic calls to see if the matches were "taking" and note any disconnections. Then someone from the Steering Committee could quietly pursue and either help overcome obstacles or make a rematch if that seemed wisest.

The Other Half of Mentoring

At the "birthing" meeting in our basement, we assumed mentoring relationships would exist as islands unto themselves. After all, that's how transformational mentoring seemed to have happened for each of us.

But a year after launching our pilot, Mentees began asking about the possibility of presentations, seminars, or other group experiences to enhance what was happening on those islands. You know by now it was mainly feedback that drove change, so as was our way, we experimented.

Dr. Michelle Robin holds a breakout session for HEMPers on health and wellness.

We had been holding a quarterly meeting for Mentors, so it seemed a similar meeting for Mentees might be a good idea. This proposal had come up before, but we had rejected it because we were overly cautious about protecting Mentees' information. They signed on with trust that there would be no loose lips about their businesses' ups and downs. Were we risking that promise by hosting them together?

No need to ask; they had expressed an interest. Next came some modest experiments, first in the form of occasional small-group lunches with presentations on key business development topics. Positive feedback deemed them a big success. Mentees let us know these experiences enhanced their learning opportunities. It was as if we had suddenly doubled the value of how we were helping by complementing the focused one-on-one connections with more broad-ranging peer mentoring.

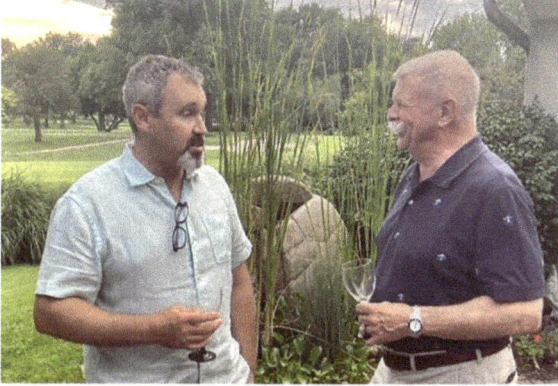

Kevin Grabill and Dan Axtell chat confidentially at a happy hour.

The Mentees helped us see what we had been missing in our caution about confidentiality. Discretion was critical, of course, but their trust in this element of HEMP was high. Perhaps as significant a need was to feel less alone in their leadership. When you start and lead a company, whom do you talk to without caution? It can't be your employees or competitors or others who might inadvertently leak information. At HEMP, these Mentees saw others doing what they were doing who would understand, commiserate, encourage, and challenge. They were no longer alone.

As soon as this became clearer, it was like a smack on the side of the head. That safe peer experience had been a major impact for many of us participating in leadership organizations. Sitting alongside others like ourselves, we could opine or ask questions or share stories with people who knew why talking things over mattered. They also understood why the information needed to be held close. We would come away with advice from others fighting the same battles we were—and with some lifelong friendships, too.

Soon these lunches and occasional group meetings morphed into more than ten programs every year. We would quickly add a social hour to each meeting to ensure there was plenty of time to interact and make new connections. Then we created an annual daylong retreat to intensify the process. These one-day getaways would become a highlight with some major attractions. We also added small groups we called "forums" so Mentees could meet regularly with the same peers to wrestle with issues in a safe setting.

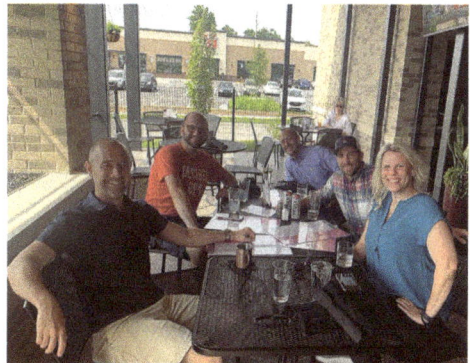

HEMP Fellows Jeff Kreutz, Andrew Cameron, Joe Beveridge, Will Buchanan and Danielle Debbrecht meet for their monthly forum.

In time, we would find as much as 50 percent of the business and personal support Mentees were receiving came from these group events. Mentors also profited from the relationships and from accessing first-rate information to challenge their businesses.

HEMP was growing and growing up. But we were far from done! Significant shifts and re-shifts lay ahead as culture drove structural changes.

Table setting at a Lunch with The Big Guy (LWTBG).

CHAPTER 5

Getting Organized

About four years into our story, I began to grow uneasy with the driving role I had assumed by default. After all, it was in *my* basement (sorry Shirley, lower level) the troop of founders convened, and since then I had been involved in nearly all of the decisions. No apologies here, as every entrepreneurial enterprise must have a committed soul behind it. New organizations are as demanding and needy as babies, and there has to be a mom or dad invested heart and soul to keep up the 3:00 a.m. feedings and bandage the scrapes as the kid learns to toddle.

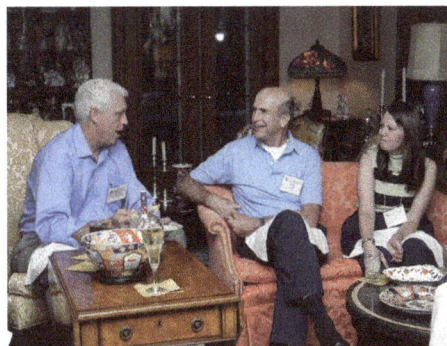

Don Proffer shares stories with Walt and Judy Rychlewski.

HEMP was making rapid headway due mostly to the quality and commitment of that initial group of founders and those they attracted to this work. We began brainstorming the "must-haves" of a, well, *organized* organization and started creating them.

A New Status

Up to now, we had operated under the legal umbrella of The Shirley and Barnett C. Helzberg, Jr. Foundation. It was time to get legal status as our own 501(c)(3). We also set up a governance structure with a three-person Executive Committee that would lead, as directed by the 501(c)(3) requirements. I became chair of the Board, and experienced mentor Bill Reisler of Kansas City Equity Partners took the role of secretary-treasurer. Linda Gill Taylor, an entrepreneurial attorney who created a staffing firm representing attorneys, became president.

Linda Gill Taylor

I explained the change in a newsletter article this way.

> *The rationale for these moves is quite simple—in the very long run when I go to my reward, I do not want HEMP seen as my hobby or an organization [that] disappears when Barnett does! Since I am a hunter more than a skinner, it is time for someone with multiple skills to institutionalize HEMP. Yes, you will still have to put up with me at meetings—but we want you to know what drove these changes.*
>
> *HEMP's start-up was a dream come true for me and far too easy due to the wonderful Mentors and Mentees and the help of so many in our community. May it ever be thus!*

Until this change, I had operated by drawing on the wisdom of what we had named the Steering Committee, which was made up of six or seven stellar leaders I would call for advice. I saw them as the brains behind all this; most were PhDs and hooked into entrepreneurship through the Kauffman Foundation or as part of the business school at UMKC. The beauty of the group was this: they understood the problems that affected small businesses, with the added element of also understanding people.

Our decision-making relationship had entrepreneurial simplicity, which allowed us to move quickly and avoid drawn-out voting processes or bureaucracy. When things came up, I would call the committee members and ask, "Is this the way to go?" and they'd steer. For those who hated committees the way I did, the time commitment asked of them was a dream. We might all meet together only once a year, and if it were more often, the agenda was clear enough we could speed through what might have been planned as a four-hour meeting in two and a half hours. In the new structure we were creating, this Steering Committee stayed on as a valuable resource, providing input and perspective as we sought them out.

Linda Gill Taylor smiling with fellow HEMP participants.

With Linda Gill Taylor taking the presidency, fresh leadership brought fresh energy. For example, she set up two new committees: one to drive programs and the other to work on developing additional funding streams. (Please recall here that I saw "committee" as a four-letter word, so even if you hadn't known my role had changed, you'd have known it with these committee announcements!)

Linda set out to improve the Mentee selection process by putting new muscle into the site visits we did at each potential Mentee's workplace before the Mentee was interviewed. Under her leadership, the

Mentor-Mentee matching process became more sophisticated. We added what looked like a night of "speed dating," during which Mentees could interview the Mentors in search of the chemistry that makes a good match.

She knew what she was doing, and my decision to withdraw from the role of president seemed smarter all the time. At the end of 1999, she wrote the following in her HEMP newsletter column:

> Perhaps the most time and care this year has been put into involving volunteers in program and event planning and strengthening the Mentee intake and matching processes. Our goal was to create a volunteer leadership cadre for HEMP's future and to achieve the highest possible percentage of effective mentoring relationships. What all of us involved in HEMP really care about is realizing Barnett's dream of helping build companies by mentoring the entrepreneurs who run them.

Who could ask for more?

Bill Eddy followed Linda Gill Taylor into the presidency and continued to move HEMP forward. His vision and support, such as helping secure office space, strengthened our organization. As dean of the UMKC Bloch School, he consistently brought sound advice as we grew.

Our next president, Doug Klink, had experience in mentoring with his leadership at the Central Exchange, the premier women's leadership development organization in Kansas City. He seamlessly led HEMP during this time of change, but unfortunately, he moved, cutting short his tenure.

Bill and Linda Eddy

Doug Klink

In fact, all who served in the presidency made a unique contribution. For instance, during his term, Bill Reisler created a resource he called Lunch with The Big Guy—aka a group luncheon with me.

The whole "The Big Guy" thing was wonderfully funny since, at first glance, it sounded like some silly attempt at aggrandizement. But on meeting me, it was easy to see it was a way to poke fun at my status as the poster boy for the vertically challenged. And it gave me a chance to publicly explain that I had to repeat kindergarten *not because I was dumb* but because I was the smallest in the class. (Later, I would begin to finish letters to HEMPers using "HEMPingly Yours, TBG"—The Big Guy—as my signature.) At these luncheons, I would get to sit down with six to eight HEMP participants and invite them to talk about their

Bill Reisler

businesses and to present their current challenges. And I had it easy! When some would ask questions, I would just respond, "Why don't we go around the room and ask these smart folks?" They would be off and running!

> ## Nobody is smart all over.

This idea to ask Mentees for the answer started with stories my dad had about his meetings with his esteemed attorney Arthur Mag. Dad always arrived with questions ready in a black book (he would often wake in the middle of the night jotting down questions in it). He would propose an issue, to which Mag would invariably respond, "What do you think you should do?" When Dad came up with his answers, Mag would respond, "Barney, that sounds good!" Later, when he saw what was happening, Dad said, "Mag, if you've got me answering my own questions, why the hell am I paying you one hundred dollars an hour?" They both laughed, but what Mag did was serious. The magic of his mentoring, and all great mentoring, was in helping the Mentee find his or her answers, not in functioning as an all-knowing consultant.

A group of HEMPers at a Lunch with The Big Guy.

> ## The magic of all great mentoring is in helping the Mentee find his or her answers, not in functioning as an all-knowing consultant.

When Walt Rychlewski became president in 2003, he came with a strong background in tech development. He saw to it that our website (which had been little more than an advertising brochure) became an interactive, useful tool.

If it appeared to Walt that our technology was behind the times, there was a reason: me. Back in 1997, when Joe Rog, the intern from UMKC who had served as our administrator, left us, we decided we would outsource administrative functions to a management company. Because the newly hired company would handle all the tasks from its office, we wouldn't have to devote time to finding new team members to do what Joe had done. This

Walt Rychlewski

mattered because in a moment that showcased that I was forward-thinking and daring, I had announced, "There'll be no computers for HEMP!" (This only reinforced my reputation as a great innovator, like the time I refused to pay an additional 20 percent fee to have Helzberg Diamonds television ads broadcast in color. "No one's going to pay for color TV," I boldly declared.) Thank goodness Walt came along.

To keep growing, HEMP needed the fresh perspectives and direction these presidents would bring! Each has come with his or her commitment to innovate and lead and made us better each year. Remember, the president of HEMP is a volunteer, a passionate, incredibly competent, and successful program participant who oversees our program and supports our managing director.

Reorganizing, Part I

We had always defined ourselves as a feedback-intensive organization. Much of that wisdom came from the founders' group: they understood entrepreneurs were by nature an independent, freewheeling, quick-to-decide crowd with a significant need to have a voice. Otherwise, many of them would have stayed in safer corporate settings that rewarded going along over striking out on their own. To keep up with our participants, we would need to check carefully and often about what was working and what wasn't in order to make adjustments, just as they were doing in their own ventures.

How we went about this feedback varied. Several times we called on our friends at the Kauffman Foundation to survey our folks. Other times we made sure feedback was an integral part of both Mentee and Mentor gatherings. Sometimes we used what we called the 3 Magic Questions, which had been suggested by Mary McElroy, a guest speaker to the MBA students I taught at Rockhurst University. When students asked her how to receive better feedback during annual performance reviews, she suggested they ask these three questions below.

The 3 Magic Questions

1. What am I doing that you like?
2. What am I doing that you do not like?
3. What am I not doing that you would like?

I thought this idea was wonderful! After we taught HEMPers the questions, a Mentee told me he had gotten a new order from a customer because he simply asked for feedback using the questions. We knew the 3 Magic Questions had power and used them for feedback regularly for HEMP programs.

In late 2004 when both Mentees and Mentors voiced negative feedback about one of the retreat speakers, we listened, especially HEMP Mentor Ray Pitman. He told us he would like to clarify the retreat feedback and also gather broader and deeper input about how the organization should be improving.

Ray Pitman leading us in singing "God Bless America."

When Ray Pitman asked for this assignment, we had already learned to pay attention. Ray came to us as a Mentor in 2001 and took to the role so enthusiastically that over time he collected his own tribe of Mentees, seventeen to be exact.

No wonder. Ray was one of a kind. He was in the US Army Corps of Engineers in World War II, stationed in the South Pacific. His team was responsible for keeping a refueling station for fighter planes operational. That meant that when the enemy bombed the airfield, Ray's platoon would need to rebuild it, and it happened over and over.

Their primary challenge was this: airplanes landed on one side of the airfield; the fuel tank was on the other. A big, cast-iron line between the two delivered the fuel to the planes. These fuel lines would be destroyed during the bombings and had to be replaced as quickly as possible. That meant digging a channel for the new fuel line, followed by eight to ten men moving that heavy line into the channel.

Ray Pitman showing Barnett C. Helzberg, Jr. his invention the "cherry picker," otherwise known as a boom lift.

In the downtime between these essential fuel-line replacements, Ray began to wonder how to speed up this critical rebuilding process. On site was a large stationary crane used to pull the fuel line off the truck that delivered it and move it to the stockpile. What if they mounted this stationary crane onto the back of a truck, then used it to pick up the heavy line and move it across the field and into position in the channel? After the war, Ray created a company to adopt this idea for industry, inventing the "cherry picker" used by every utility company and tree-trimming service and a thousand other enterprises. We knew what happened when Ray Pitman committed himself to a project.

HEMPers enjoy visiting one another's businesses to learn about their culture and history. Here we strap in to test out the "cherry picker," which Ray Pitman invented.

Some thought the HEMP feedback search Ray was describing was too time-intensive for someone of his talent and stature, but he insisted and went to work. And work he did! Over the next few months, Ray called participants to ask them what we could be doing better. He then asked each of them to send their feedback to him in writing. This feedback came from Mentees, Mentors, and Fellows. By year's end, he presented the Board with a three-ring binder, collecting what he had heard plus a set of recommendations for how HEMP should respond. Thorough he was; passive he wasn't.

His major, and perhaps most controversial, recommendation dealt with changing our organizational structure. HEMPers had told him they would like to play a more significant role in decisions. He recommended creating several "buckets of responsibilities," which became our different committees. He also recommended changing our administrative structure away from the typical executive director model most organizations like ours used. He believed this committee structure would support HEMP better by having our participants actively invested in running our organization. This would eliminate the "funnel problem" of ideas and issues getting stuck where one person is responsible for everything.

Ray found that executive directors often carried both decision-making authority and burden that should belong to the volunteers. He wanted to create several committee chair positions that focused on key areas of HEMP: Finance, Mentors, Mentees, Fellows, Programs, Marketing, Strategic Planning, and the like. Otherwise, how would ownership grow? Instead of having an executive director, a paid team member would serve as managing director, tasked with implementing participants' decisions.

Organizational Chart

```
                    ┌──────────────┐
                    │   Board of   │
                    │  Directors   │
                    └──────┬───────┘
                           │
                    ┌──────┴───────┐
                    │  President   │
                    └──────┬───────┘
                           │
   ┌───────────┬───────────┼───────────┬───────────┐
┌──────┐  ┌──────────┐ ┌──────────┐ ┌─────────────┐
│Finance│ │President-│ │ Managing │ │ Measurement │
│       │ │  Elect   │ │ Director │ │             │
└───────┘ └──────────┘ └──────────┘ └─────────────┘
```

Mentor Chair	Mentee Chair	Fellows Chair	Program Chair	Marketing (PR/Web) Chair
Steering Committee	Steering Committee	Steering Committee	Steering Committee	Steering Committee
Mentor Recruitment Mentor Training Mentor/Mentee Assignment Evaluation of Mentor/Mentee Progress Mentors	Mentee Recruitment Mentee Orientation Successful Mentor/Mentee Relationship Develop Class Pride	Create and Develop New Forums Mentor/Mentee Awareness Program Mentee Buddy System	Educational Programs for 1-2-3 Year Mentees General Membership Programs Breakfast Events Networking Events LWTBG Retreat	Suggest fresh ideas for and maintain the website Develop and present a community image for HEMP

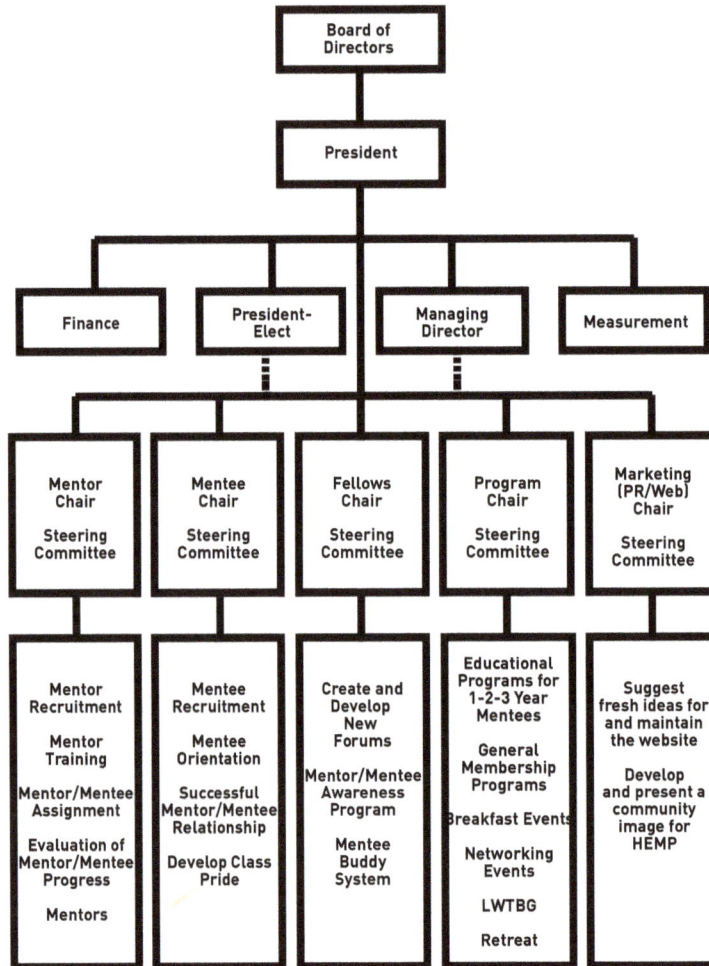

Ray's original organizational chart for HEMP.

I'll just say it. For some of us, such criticisms of the committee structure as "excessive," "unnecessarily complicated," and "overblown" came pretty quickly. We saw ourselves as a relatively small organization after all. By adopting Ray's proposed structure, were we going to wind up with more board members than participants?

Walt Rychlewski was HEMP president at the time and came to the role with a load of experience as an engineer, a serial entrepreneur who started not one but six successful businesses, and then a university professor and dean. He knew the power of lean and mean, put in the structure you need to get the job done but no more. And he imagined HEMP doing the same. Even when he led the move to re-create our online presence, he created a task force that would disband when the website was implemented and functioning well. No ongoing technology committee. Just see the need, assign resources, complete the job, and move on.

In the for-profit world, differences of opinion like this between Ray Pitman and Walt Rychlewski are managed by using the "buck stops here" definition a single arbitrator must render a thumbs-up or thumbs-down and accept full responsibility for what follows—in other words, one wins, one loses.

But that isn't how this difference of opinion got resolved. Instead, Ray and Walt went one-on-one and talked. They pushed each other, and they argued. But mostly they listened well. One of our people would later say, "Two honorable men with strongly different solutions went to the mat. But because they were honorable and dealt with each other respectfully, the result was not just a good solution but an authentic friendship between them." No gamesmanship or backdoor manipulations were used to ambush the other—just respectful pushing and listening. It was how we hoped big decisions here would come about, and these two men had shown us a grand example.

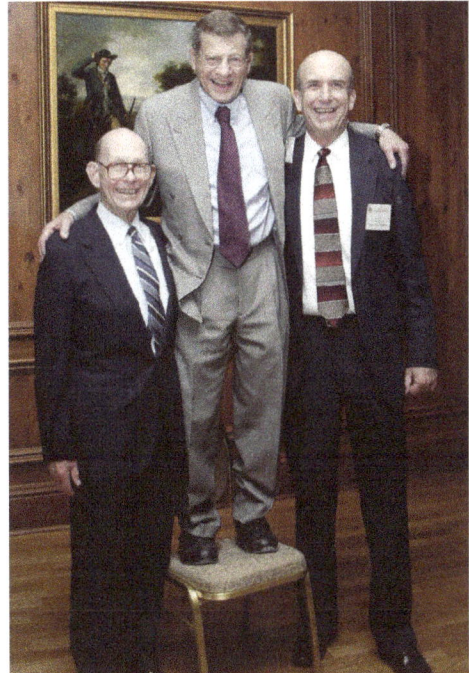

Barnett, with Ray Pitman and Walt Rychlewski, proves that he's the biggest guy in the room.

When all was said and done, the Board decided to follow Ray's recommendation, and Walt supported the decision.

Here's the caveat. Ray wasn't just about getting his way—ever. He then stepped in to do the work it would take to implement this change! Ray was retired from his successful business by this time. If he hadn't been, retirement would have been a necessity because he was sometimes working sixty hours a week for HEMP, setting up new lines of communication, creating processes, and working with managing director Christina Dreiling to develop ways to support these systems.

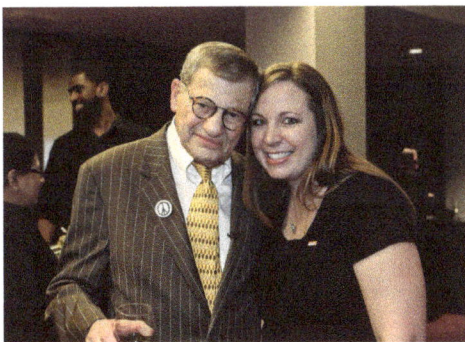

Barnett C. Helzberg, Jr. and Christina Dreiling, HEMP managing director.

Christina came to the organization in 2003 and proved her value very quickly. Ray promoted her from program coordinator to managing director during this organizational transition. As of the writing of this book, she is still our managing director, and we are incredibly fortunate to have her. Christina has a lot of autonomy in her role because she has earned it. She always practices good judgment and has a great sense of confidentiality. She and her associates, Haley Young and Maggie Johnson, are top-quality people and are the ones who keep our participants happy. We have all grown together.

To introduce the new organizational structure, Ray started a round of small-group lunches of six to eight people—maybe twenty lunches in all—to explain and get feedback on the idea. Ray was everywhere, and because of the heroic work he did to implement his recommendation, the value began to appear sooner rather than later.

Fairly quickly, we could see that greater participant involvement in decisions and directions meant greater ownership. If things weren't getting done in the executive director model we were using previously, the executive director was to blame. In the new model, the weight of HEMP's culture, direction, and strategy rested squarely on the shoulders of our participants to make every aspect successful.

Maybe a more important outcome of this collaborative decision was the talent-development pool the committee system provided in which to grow future HEMP board and committee members. You come to believe in causes you sweat for—and HEMPers needed to commit as true believers so the organization could continue to improve.

Jim and Gina Stuelke cozy up with Ray Pitman.

Ray was easy to follow because he always seemed to be looking ahead and looking out for everyone. For example, back when the "Good Ol' Boys Club" was too often evident in business, Ray started a "Good Ol' Girls Club," and invited HEMP women to join! I saw Ray's contributions as incredibly powerful. Indeed, we would joke together at HEMP gatherings about changing the name of the organization to the Pitman Entrepreneurial Mentoring Program. However, our acronym would then become PEMP—well, no. Too close to that other four-letter P word for anyone's comfort! It was a laugh we all enjoyed together.

Ray Pitman shows off his special gift from Barnett, a squawky rubber chicken.

Ray's contributions changed HEMP in a way I could never have imagined. We were all so grateful, and I wanted to present him with a very special gift at our annual Schmoozefest event in front of all our HEMPers, which numbered about 150 in attendance. I expressed my sincere gratitude in words I can't recall and then handed him the gift, which was wrapped in beautiful gold paper and finished with a bow. Ray, with an emotional expression on his face, opened the gift to see it was a rubber squawking chicken. His expression immediately turned to laughter. But it was Ray who had the last laugh. Many times, I received a telephone call or voicemail from that damn chicken squawking in my ear.

Reorganizing, Part II

In many organizations, the power most often lies with who decides to commit and what they bring. Although you do your best to attract the finest, whether they come and when they come aren't neat cause-and-effect occurrences. When they do happen, however, stars collide.

Ray Pitman followed Walt Rychlewski into the presidency, followed by Lirel Holt, a HEMP founder and committed Mentor. It was Lirel's business experience that solidified Ray's work and jetted us forward. Lirel had been CEO of CARSTAR, a remarkable business he had created as a network of franchised and company-owned collision repair shops. When he sold controlling interest in 1997, it was the largest collision repair franchise in the world, with 350 stores in North America. Because of his experience honing and capturing systems so they would be transferable to franchisees, he offered to do the same for HEMP.

Lirel Holt

We weren't planning to franchise, but we would have been fools to say no to an expert investing his time and resources into improving our practices and moving them online. That way, he explained, we would have consistency and clarity for the future. He also believed owners should always be ready to sell or franchise their business; that perspective keeps focus clear on what matters. We were in and informally called the project, "How to run HEMP if, God forbid, Christina gets hit by a bus or decides to have triplets (though she claims she'd rather be hit by a bus)."

Lirel and Christina spent *two years* on this venture, talking over how each piece of Christina's job gets done. They codified it and moved it into a software management platform Lirel had designed. Lirel and Christina applied the MAP (marketing, administration, and product/service) evaluation process to HEMP. Through reading Michael Gerber's *The E-Myth Revisited* and doing the MAP evaluation, we were able to identify and articulate clearly all of our processes. It was similar to a detailed strategic-planning documentation exercise that anyone could read and follow. Lirel also very generously designed and contributed software that would allow both Mentors and Mentees to report on their meetings electronically. These software designs became an immense gift to HEMP and are known as HEMP's Operating System.

Once we were working on the Operating System, we came up with the idea of a certified Mentor as a way to honor Mentors and attract Mentees. As with many of our good ideas, this one became a reality. We created an online training tool to certify and communicate our values to our Mentors. We realized a customized Mentee version of this onboarding training program would be another great addition.

We came out of this season of reorganizing stronger and better equipped to serve the cause of providing first-class mentoring to entrepreneurs.

Moving On

At the end of Lirel's two-year term, Chuck Hoffman took over as president, and he ensured that we were able to put the things in place that we needed to operate. It took Chuck's leadership to add the right processes to make the new organizational structure effective and efficient. Efficiency is always important to our lean organization focused on serving our mentees.

In our fifteenth year in business, with close to 200 active participants, we were leasing office space in a UMKC building at 4747 Troost Avenue. Bill Eddy had invited us to use this affordable space, and up until this point, it had served us well. However, due to our growth, we were now hosting meetings in which HEMPers were sitting on the tops of desks and chairs were crowded as close together as we could manage. Although this arrangement was conducive to togetherness, it was not conducive to good learning and decision-making.

Chuck Hoffman

While meetings were held at the Troost location, programs and events were held at hotel meeting spaces and country clubs. The cost and administrative hassle of keeping on top of multiple locations and arrangements was considerable. Christina ran the numbers and told us we would be better off both logistically and financially finding a larger home for HEMP.

The 4747 Troost Office

So, we shopped Kansas City real estate, which proved incredibly time-consuming. Our expectation was that we would find a location on the Country Club Plaza, Kansas City's premier shopping and business district, but it turned out to be too expensive. We decided to expand our search to two smaller districts with more affordable amenities, the River Market and Crossroads. At that time, Crossroads was a developing area, but not many people were familiar with it. We looked at a number of buildings in the Crossroads, and then finally, a year into the search, we found a downtown space near Nineteenth and Main that was interesting, accessible, and about the right size. It was large enough to fit our needs, and the leasing price was more workable than the spaces we had seen on the Plaza. Although it looked like two separate buildings from the outside, once inside, a common entry area with mailboxes connected the two. Because the buildings shared a central exterior lounge area, and the office windows looked right out onto that space, we made it clear to the building owner that the lessee for the other building would need to be a good complement for the all-about-business atmosphere we wanted to establish. That made sense to her, so we signed on and started renovations.

The Baltimore Avenue entrance to HEMP's office and Barnett's Basement.

But this turned out to be a moment where dealing in diamonds rather than commercial property leasing did not serve me well. One day, a short man with a ready smile popped in our door and stuck out his hand. "Hi, I'm Flo," he said. "And I'm your new neighbor."

Our new neighbor owned a nightclub featuring performances by drag queens. He let us know there would be dancing in the area above our offices and his performers would want to use our common mail area as their dressing space. Some business atmosphere!

Clearly, this wasn't going to work. With encouragement from our attorney, the owner kindly let us out of our lease. We moved on to find a space just one block over at 2000 Baltimore Avenue in a beautiful older building that was in the process of being gutted and remodeled. We would be able to create our own design for the space we chose, and the location near Kansas City's historic Union Station felt right. After two years of searching, with luck on our side this time, the historic Crossroads District became the perfect area for our office, centrally located and in the middle of many landmark restaurants.

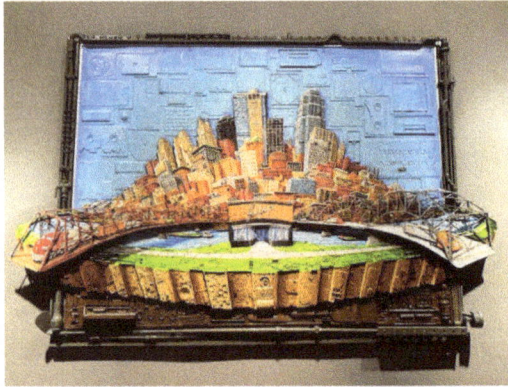

Artwork created to celebrate HEMP's 20th anniversary using only items donated by HEMPers that represent their businesses. Items ranged from telephones to calculators to microphones.

Moving in was a celebration, partly because of the open, airy, modern new space, but also because of how many HEMPers had jumped in to donate their professional skills to get the design and construction right. We had office spaces, a generous conference room, a fully equipped kitchen area, and an open central area to meet and kibbitz. And yes, computers were definitely part of the design!

We were as excited and proud as a young couple with their first home and threw a big open house with three hundred guests. We invited not only HEMPers but also vendors and the community—a whole batch of people! Our landlord, Charlie Barnard, a manufacturer of socks, even showed up with socks adorned with the HEMP logo for everyone.

About ten years later, we also leased and renovated a good-size meeting room in the building's lower level. This provided a home for programs and events, greatly lessening our need to rent hotel meeting space and giving us a place where the design and visuals were uniquely HEMP. The Executive Committee dubbed it "Barnett's Basement" in a well-crafted reminder of HEMP's simple beginnings. My first and only wife, Shirley, still calls it our lower level whenever she comes to events.

With a renovated and solidified organizational structure and our new home, we were ready to wrangle with what growth would mean.

The new HEMP office located at 2000 Baltimore Avenue.

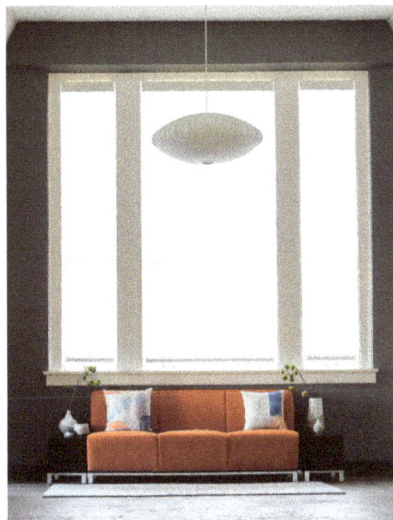

Part 4: Is Bigger Better?

(2010–2018)

HEMPers share business issues at Lunch with The Big Guy.

CHAPTER 6

Making HEMP Bigger

S ince entrepreneurial was our middle name, the idea occasionally surfaced from participants and other organizations to consider taking this proven experience and sharing it more widely.

I was never personally interested in organizational expansion. Still, I did like the idea of sharing what we learned with others. In this spirit, I approached Jack Welch, famed, and recently retired CEO of General Electric, to pique his interest in a HEMP-like program. I never intended for us to run it. I was simply offering the idea and our support. My letter said the following:

Networking is so important as an entrepreneur so we created an event called Schmooze Fest solely to give people that opportunity.

> *Dear Mr. Welch: As a good manager wannabe, I've followed your wonderful career for many years! I've also followed the stories of your retirement, and it looks like it will be a second career rather than retirement. I guarantee it will be as much fun as the first.*
>
> *I thought that the mentoring program that we have set up might be of interest and that you might consider your version in your area. I am therefore enclosing information. If we can be of any help at all in this effort, we would be most pleased to do so.*

He graciously responded with this handwritten note:

> *Dear Mr. Helzberg: Thank you so much for your note and program. Congratulations on a great vision. I appreciate your offer to help and will keep it in mind as my plans develop.*

Ralph Wrobley

When retired attorney Ralph Wrobley was president of HEMP, he made sure conversations about expansion were on the docket. Ralph had worked at law firm Husch Blackwell with high-end, large-scale clients. He came to us with the business conviction that if a company isn't growing, it's dying. Ralph thought it was important for us to measure the growth of the Mentees as they went through our program. We also needed to measure how HEMP was supporting Kansas City so we could use that in our marketing materials. We started to track our participants' revenue and employee growth over their three-year term. The results were impressive.

43%
INCREASE IN REVENUE GROWTH

41%
INCREASE IN EMPLOYEE COUNT

CONTRIBUTED MORE THAN
$748M
TO THE KANSAS CITY COMMUNITY

Average Mentee results after completing the three-year program.

Interest from Others

As early as 2000, we began getting inquiries from entrepreneurs in St. Louis and North Carolina about duplicating the process we had created to mentor business owners. We were excited and flattered by the recognition and interest from others and had a sincere desire to help them start their own programs.

In 2004, successful Oklahoma City businessman Tom Love of Love's Travel Stop expressed an interest in learning more about our mentoring program. We invited him to Kansas City for a conversation. It was a great visit, but in time he would choose to partner with a university, a more manageable model for structure, resource sharing, and sponsorship.

Coaching from Michie Slaughter, a leader in the Kauffman Foundation, emphasized the importance of sticking close to HEMP's original approach if we chose to partner with another mentoring program. He described that founder role as providing staying power and personal involvement for at least four to five years until the new organization was steady on its feet.

In 2008, we began to think we had found just such a situation. Andy Lawlor, a presenter from the University of Michigan we had used several times, put us in contact with Mike Jandernoa, a successful businessman in Grand Rapids. Mike had been CEO and chairman of the board of Perrigo, a global pharmaceutical company. He expressed an interest in beginning a mentoring program in western Michigan with some of the same motivations that had energized me, mainly wanting to grow business success.

At our invitation, Mike came to Kansas City twice. He brought with him a team, some of whom were from the University of Michigan and had expressed an interest in sponsorship. We talked in depth about the HEMP program and the resources we might provide. Mike responded by sending his private jet to ferry several of us to western Michigan so we could continue conversations. His interest was genuine.

Later, Mike's team sent their administrator to Kansas City to work with Christina for a week, job shadowing and learning, attending a Mentee site-visit day, and much more. With Lirel Holt's blessing, we sketched out a licensing agreement to provide them access to HEMP's Operating System. HEMP may franchise after all!

However, what started as a smooth beginning would become bumpier as we realized we were taking too much time away from our Kansas City participants. We had a small staff, and the time Christina was on the phone helping Grand Rapids could be helping HEMPers. We needed to focus on Kansas City.

Rethinking Bigger

More careful thought finally led us to bless Mike Jandernoa in his Jandernoa Entrepreneurial Mentoring (JEM) venture without being directly involved and feel gladness we had been able to share resources to assist. We have stayed in touch with JEM and have found we can now learn from each other!

A few years later, the Kauffman Foundation approached us about including HEMP in its catalog of offerings and perhaps even franchising it globally. We were flattered by the interest, so I called Ted Cohn, a wise and experienced mentor of mine, to talk it over.

"I have one question," he said thoughtfully. "Does it help Mentees?"

The fog of flattery cleared immediately when Ted Cohn asked that simple question. We built mentoring success on relationships and community, and these take time and personal connections to develop and maintain. No, joining Kauffman wouldn't help Mentees! We didn't proceed.

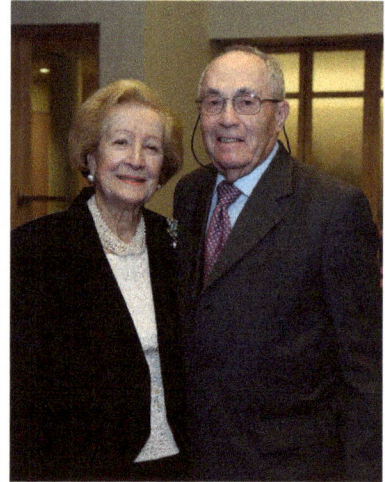

Alice and Ted Cohn

66 Does it help Mentees? 99

This simple question, "Does it help Mentees?" is so significant we painted it on our conference room wall, and we often look at it to guide us as we make important decisions.

In the middle of this reflection, Vivien Jennings of Rainy Day Books, a Kansas City independent bookstore, said to me, "I look at expansion this way: Bigger isn't better; better is better."

Bigger isn't better; better is better. Our thoughts went immediately to the expansion venture we were developing. We were pursuing this because we assumed more is always better. But is it?

66 Bigger isn't better; better is better. 99

We immediately began looking at expansion with new eyes. The financial demands on HEMP, and particularly the demands on our team members and volunteer time, would be high. Had we thought through all of the implications of stretching our resources in this way? How might it impact the vision and mission we were already pursuing?

With a new focus on better, we could now choose to put bigger in its proper place. We did offer coaching to two local Kansas City organizations, the University of Kansas Medical Center, as they established a mentoring program for doctors, and JE Dunn, a large construction enterprise with an internal mentoring program. So, we never gave up the idea of assisting others and sharing what we were doing. We just aren't willing to operate other mentoring programs beyond HEMP.

In 2012, we combined bigger and better in a way that fit us. We wrote a book—a "mentoring Bible"—in which we shared what we had learned about successful Mentor-Mentee relationships by showcasing twenty-two stories. It also offered key templates we had developed through the years to aid selection, training, and program development for mentoring programs. *Entrepreneurs + Mentors = Success* was our way of sharing with the world what we had learned and accomplished.

The book found a ready audience in university business programs. For example, it was embraced by Washington University in St. Louis, Saint Louis University, and Wichita State University as a part of their curriculum. Through that venture, we saw that "bigger" can mean many things besides numerical growth if "better" is kept clearly in view.

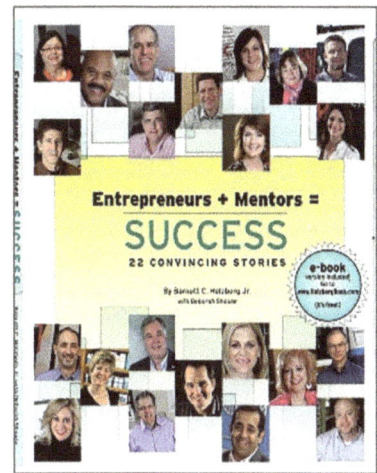

Entrepreneurs + Mentors = Success book tour.

Christina and I traveled to each university to speak to their students as a wrap-up to their semester. On each trip, we took a Mentor-Mentee pair that was featured in the book. When we visited Saint Louis University, we had a calamity of errors—illness, valet accidents, broken-down rental cars, a few tears, and a few more cuss words. At the end of the day, during a much-needed break over a drink or two, we moved on to laughter. Through that day's madness, the four of us were able to get to know each other better and realized how valuable that type of experience would be for other HEMPers.

On our way home, we remembered participant Danny O'Neill had just been to the Zappos headquarters, where he had a very educational and motivating experience. We called Danny to discuss it and decided we were going to host a HEMP field trip to Las Vegas. HEMP's annual entrepreneurial field trip was born. As of this writing, HEMP has taken eight entrepreneurial field trips to different cities, including Reykjavik, Iceland!

Mentee Selection Committee discussing Mentee prospects on the bus between site visits.

CHAPTER 7

Making HEMP Better

F ast-forward to 2011. It's fine to declare that we are committed to better not bigger, but we needed to get to work to show what better could mean for HEMP in this adolescence of our growth.

Improving Integration

Training for Mentors and Mentees

From day one, we had operated under the assumption that Mentors pretty much knew what they were doing. They had succeeded in running major businesses after all, which made it a safe bet. Most seemed to take naturally to the role of asking questions rather than giving answers, and their considerable success led them to ask the right, best questions to move Mentees forward.

Dan McDougal

We had our online training tool for Mentors, but we were coming to understand it was taking too long for the first year of the relationship to become productive. One Mentee told us with regret, "I didn't get much from the first year." We saw this delay as a waste of great resources. With some research, we realized we needed to help our Mentors and Mentees connect expeditiously.

Our president at that time was Dan McDougal. Dan was the first HEMP Mentee who went on to become a Mentor and later president, so he offered a unique perspective. With ten years in HEMP under his belt, he knew which recurring issues needed addressing. Under Dan's leadership, the HEMP dictionary was written so we were all speaking the same language. Additionally, to address our problems with relationship building during the first year, the Mentor Boot Camp was created.

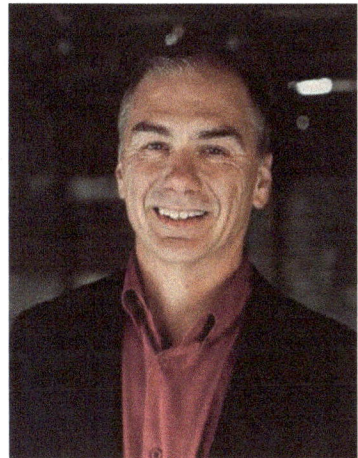

The Mentor Boot Camp (a binder given to Mentors and an annual training session) provided training primarily aimed at the first ninety days of the Mentor-Mentee relationship. It helped Mentors understand what to do in what order, what assignments to give, and which questions made the most difference.

A Mentee program called Jumpstart (again a binder and training session) gave the Mentees the same advantage. We began to seed ideas like suggesting Mentees come to the first meeting with their Mentor with a completed analysis of the strengths, weaknesses, opportunities, and threats (SWOT) of their business. The Jumpstart tool helped with setting expectations and knowing how to schedule meetings with Mentors along with other practical information. Now both Mentors and Mentees could hit the ground running.

Mentees were also assigned a Fellow as a Mentee Buddy to assist in the process of getting things going, while new Mentors got help from a Mentor Buddy, an experienced Mentor in HEMP. These additional resources met with their assigned partner a couple of times and continued to be available on an as-needed basis.

Earlier Assessment of Potential Mentors

As a follow-on to our new training methods, we put more effort into clarifying the actual process of Mentor selection. Mentors had had to apply and interview since the beginning of HEMP. At the start, I knew nearly all of them personally, however, as I had simply invited business acquaintances who demonstrated a capacity to listen and help and had good business acumen. I had never personally participated in Mentor interviews because I didn't want to interfere in a process where many of my friends and colleagues were applying. I was confident that HEMP would select the right Mentors for our organization.

As we grew, the need for Mentors grew, and awareness of this mentoring opportunity spread. We were glad to receive interest from experienced businesspeople who wanted to be a part. However, this raised a question: How could we work as hard to choose the right fit in Mentors as we had been doing with Mentees?

One impetus for finding an answer lay in my own mentoring experience. I was a champion of mentoring and enthusiastically signed on to mentor. But after a situation I mishandled in which I delivered bad advice, I fired myself as a Mentor for several years. I would later try it again, but now with Chuck Hoffman and Ralph Wrobley, two excellent Mentor partners. We learned from my experience that careful Mentor screening could help protect both Mentees and Mentors from experiences like mine.

The process we developed involved an application, a behavioral evaluation, and then an interview with the Mentor Selection Committee. We were at first pleased to see how seriously potential Mentors took this interview. For example, when the committee met with one candidate, he was visibly nervous. "This is harder than it looks," he confessed. "I haven't been to a job interview in thirty years."

We continued to improve our process by creating Mentor guidelines with our mentor chair and later president, Tracy Lockton. These guidelines are a set of skills and characteristics that describe what it takes to be a strong Mentor. After a candidate completed an application, the managing director talked with the Mentor applicant, asking questions to look for alignment with our Mentor guidelines. If the responses indicated there was likely a fit, the candidate continued to the behavioral evaluation and formal interview. If not, the process concluded there as graciously as possible.

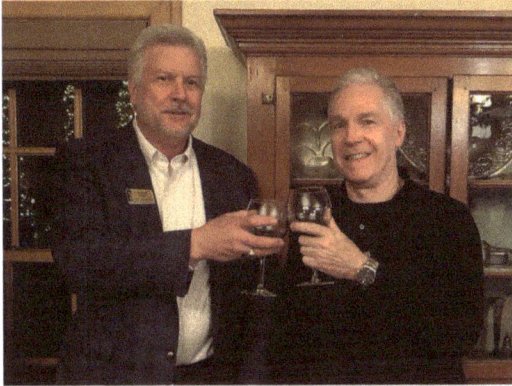

Mentors Dave Bartel and Mike O'Malley toast at a Mentor Holiday Happy Hour.

Mentors Larry Hawks, John Goodman and Robin Royals chatting.

Mentor Supports

We had ramped up training for Mentors and now wanted to create more peer networking opportunities for them as well. Mentor chair Tracy Lockton hosted a Mentors' holiday happy hour in her home. She intended for Mentors to meet other Mentors so they would see themselves as part of a group, just as the Mentees did within their Mentee class. The happy hour was also a good recruiting tool for new Mentors. It has been so successful that we now do it annually.

Mentor Scott King addressing guests at a Mentor event.

We also host periodic Mentor roundtables, smaller group conversations that let Mentors share best practices and ask questions. These Mentor meetings have become a highlight, providing ongoing training, and addressing challenges that we didn't anticipate. In a recent roundtable, one Mentor confessed to his peers, "Hearing how involved you all are with your Mentee is telling me to get on the stick. I think I've been slacking off a little, but that's going to change."

As an aside, all this focus on selecting and equipping Mentors sometimes causes people to ask if we've ever considered paying them. My answer is a resounding no. The result might have been like that of a community blood bank that wondered, "If we get so many donors while offering no compensation, how many more would we get if we paid them?" They tried offering payment, and the numbers of blood donors tanked!

Business leaders at the level of our Mentors will do remarkable work as a way to give—work that might never draw them if it felt like a job. If we did pay what their help is worth, we would be shelling out checks for hundreds of thousands of dollars regularly! They give because they've been given to and want to help others build.

We have found through the years that many of our mentors value the experience as much as we value them. For example, one day at the gym, a woman I was chatting with asked if I knew Bob Brush. I did, of course. Bob was a retired Hallmark executive, visible in community service around Kansas City, and an outstanding HEMP Mentor. She commented, "He often speaks about how much he enjoys the mentoring experience."

Improving Selections

Improving Site Visits

In our earliest years, potential Mentees would simply show up at the office for interviews, following the custom of most business interviews. After Mentees were selected and matched with a Mentor, Mentors were encouraged to make their first appointment a site visit to the Mentee's workplace.

Later, as we studied what other organizations like ours were doing, we noticed that one went to the applicant's business for an initial interview. We had instead been bringing them into our office, but when we recalled how Mentors talked with enthusiasm about how much their understanding of the Mentee grew by seeing the business, we realized this site visit could serve the selection committee well. We began to visit potential Mentees to interview them in their own setting. The process we had used initially was like trying to choose an architect

The selection committee outside a prospective Mentee's site visit.

without having ever seen anything she or he had designed. After a couple of rounds of this improved procedure, we wondered why we had ever done it any other way.

Now we were learning ways to improve our preparation for the site visits. For example, when people applied to be either Mentees or Mentors for HEMP, they would be asked to complete a behavioral evaluation. This provided a way to discuss questions of fit more objectively.

The on-site interview process was an evolution that started with a few of us in a car going to each site visit. It evolved to be a larger group, our Mentee Selection Committee, being driven in one van, sorting through reams of paper applications and eating a sack lunch. The real magic happened when we began to hire a chauffeur-driven limo bus—it was nice to have the extra room and not have one of us behind the wheel. To be as efficient as possible and use everyone's time wisely, we start early in the morning. Of course, coffee, breakfast, and lunch are provided. It's a long day, so Christina packs a customized goodie bag for every participant. In my goodie bag is an extra shirt because she knows I am bound to spill something on the one I am wearing.

Mentee Interviews

In those Mentee interviews, we continued to make sure a variety of people were involved in the selection because each of us comes at it with a different view. For example, after completing one of the interviews, most of us felt like something was a little off. The young business owner looked great on paper, but no one seemed able to define our shared caution. Were we reading too much into this whole "gut feeling" business? As we walked out together, one of the team said, "We shouldn't choose her. She doesn't like her business or her people."

We stopped to review what the interviewee had said. Since our conclusion wasn't unanimous, one of the team offered to have coffee with her to probe more deeply. When he finally asked if she enjoyed the business, she said, "No, but I've got to do it." She had taken over management because she felt her husband was running things into the ground, and her oversight would be the only way they would survive. "I'm not sure I'd be a good fit for your program," she concluded. "I doubt I'd even listen to what you tell me."

If we'd had one or two interviewers, we would have missed it, but there is wisdom in numbers and insight from diverse viewpoints. We intentionally choose a group of ten to twelve HEMP participants, ensuring we have a mix of men and women of various ages and experiences. The current president, finance chair, and managing director are always a part of the selection team. Christina has, of course, created a packed but well-thought-out schedule and seen to all the details.

On our way to the next interview, we debate our impressions of the business we have just seen and if we think the entrepreneur and HEMP would be a good fit. After a particularly lively day of these debates, a site-visit committee member said, "That was like an MBA in a day!"

Along with improving our interviews, we began working harder at a different kind of evaluation. We started taking more of a macro look at Mentees who seemed to thrive in the program versus those who didn't. We would ask one another, "What is it about that person that makes the program work so well?" For those with different results, what was it that kept them from making that all important fit?

The Mentee selection committee's many adventures on site visits.

We used this information to help evaluate and better select the interview questions. Much went well in past years because interviewers were often people with thirty to forty years of business experience and decades of work with HEMP. If those two factors were no longer in play, we would want to move more quickly from intuition to actual tested questions that helped us make successful Mentee choices.

For example, we have learned this is a useful question: "How would your spouse or significant other rank you on your listening skills? Choose a number from one to ten, and you can't use seven." Our participants with marketing experience have told us that in surveys, seven is a "cop-out" number. It's just high enough that you don't look bad, but not so high that you look arrogant. We've learned to pay careful attention to answers for questions like this one because if you can't listen, you aren't mentorable.

> 66 **If you can't listen, you aren't mentorable.** 99

Only One Mentee per Business

In the beginning, no one thought about a couple who co-ran a business wanting to participate, so when we received requests from couples, we decided to give it a try. This was an experiment, of course, because we had already declared that only the ultimate decision-maker in a business was eligible. Could this be a reasonable exception?

Once again, the "one-foot-in-the-water" principle for testing new ideas proved useful. Deborah Young, PhD was HEMP president and an organizational consultant who had come to HEMP initially because of her valuable contribution to the Marion Laboratories with Mr. K. We listened when she described mentoring one of our couples. In the end, she had to tell them, "You don't need a mentor; you need a divorce attorney!" Deborah knew counseling and knew mentoring, and she knew when to draw a line between the two.

Deborah Young, PhD

This confusion between a business partnership and a personal partnership showed up more than once, so we had to conclude we weren't counselors. The dual-company-leaders model was beyond HEMP's scope. We decided not to exclude companies with shared leadership, but we would ask them to name just one partner for mentoring through HEMP and confirm they were the Ultimate Decision-Maker, or UDM.

No Cold Turndowns

Back in my early diamond-peddling days, my dad modeled a powerful principle. He called it "no cold turndowns." That meant you don't tell a customer you don't have what they are seeking; you look for a way to suggest an alternative.

> ❝ **'No cold turndowns.' You don't tell a customer you don't have what they are seeking; you find an alternative.** ❞

HEMP took on that same spirit as we interviewed Mentees. As each interview process progressed, we worked hard to offer questions and feedback on the business that might be useful, whether the interviewee joined the program or not. If an individual wasn't accepted, we did all we could to suggest alternative places for help, such as the Kauffman FastTrac program for newer entrepreneurs. Sometimes we would send a team of Mentors to meet with the interviewee a couple of times to give outside perspective on a particular problem that had surfaced.

Walt Rychlewski combined his academic and entrepreneurial skills to help develop a yearlong instructional program that would, in time, become ScaleUp. This would later become a regular offering through the University of Missouri–Kansas City Small Business Development Center. HEMP used it as a "farm club" to coach newer business owners who did not yet qualify for our program but were ready to learn.

Lirel Holt had created an excellent business evaluation resource for 3M, a two-day course he called MAP (the program he and Christina used to develop HEMP's Operating System). It helped participants look objectively at their business growth and needs. He had adapted some of this material for presenting at HEMP retreats, and it always got stellar reviews. Later, we heard some of the Fellows talking about their frustration with a stagnating business plan. "I need to reignite," one said. In response, Lirel's program was renamed AMPUp (Administration, Marketing, Product/Services) and has become a rich resource adjunct to HEMP's formal mentoring. For us, this became another resource we could recommend to those who didn't become Mentees.

A two-day AMPUp session.

Lirel Holt showing his infamous magic trick with wine corks.

One session of AMPUp graduates.

Refining Programs

Entrepreneurial Field Trips

After our book promotional trip to Saint Louis University, we initiated what was to become an annual entrepreneurial field trip. Traveling to another city, we would see and hear firsthand from successful businesses and learn about their culture. In 2013, our team organized our first multiday trip for twenty HEMPers and spouses/significant others to Las Vegas to get an inside look at Zappos and the Shelby American automotive factory.

We chose Zappos because many of us had read the book *Delivering Happiness*, written by then-CEO Tony Hsieh, and the company was offering free tours to anyone who had read it. (Remember how I love a great deal?) Lirel Holt hooked us up with the Shelby American factory for a personalized tour. As we had hoped, the trip proved to offer enough learning, fun, and unstructured time together that relationships grew, and vulnerability got easier. In the years that followed, we would offer group visits in cities to tour Tesla, Salesforce, Starbucks, Boeing, Amazon, IBM, Yeti, Whole Foods Market, Medtronic, Kendra Scott, Visir, and more. Along with these big-name operations, we also always include visits to companies whose size more nearly matches those of our participants. These site visits got us packing off to Vegas, Nashville, San Francisco, Seattle, Minneapolis, Austin, and Iceland.

HEMPers visiting Yeti in Austin, TX.

The trips became very popular. All our HEMP participants need to do is show up. Our managing director takes care of the logistics for the trip, including transportation, dinners, hotel, and entertainment. We receive an agenda detailing which companies we will visit and when. She talks with the companies in advance so they know who will be attending and what we are interested in learning.

Many of the companies we visit come to our attention because someone in HEMP knows someone there. This often leads to us coming away with a personalized and vibrant learning experience. Behind-the-scenes tours have become the norm. Once we even met with a team of vice presidents at Starbucks and were invited to try a new special coffee blend they were creating. I didn't have three cups like I did the night I met Danny O'Neill, but it was still great. Each field trip is truly a five-star educational and relationship-building experience.

Back in 1995, I never would have pictured HEMP taking such diverse adventures. But in my mind, this was some of what "better" meant for us.

Las Vegas

Zappos
Shelby American, Inc.

Nashville

The Bluebird Café
Tennessee Bun Company
Dave Ramsey
Starstruck Music Studio

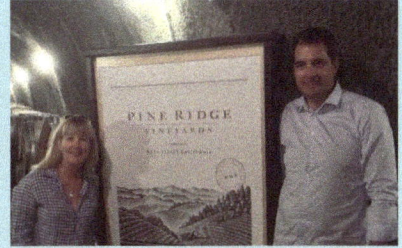

San Francisco

Praetorian Digital
Tesla
Salesforce
Pine Ridge Vineyards

Seattle

Space Needle
Starbucks
Amazon
Boeing

Minneapolis

Prince's Paisley Park
3M Innovation Center
Medtronic
The Nerdery & Prime

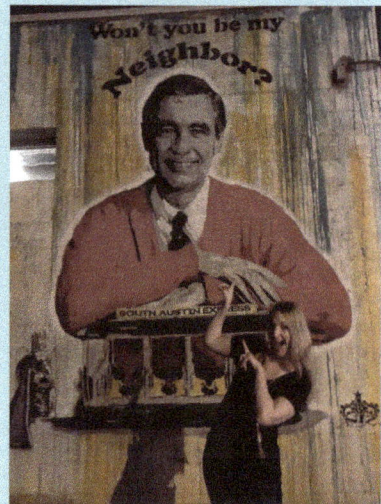

Austin

Kendra Scott
Whole Foods
Yeti

Iceland

Visir
Marel
Hellisheiðarvirkjun

Many more adventures to come!

Programs and Services

Programs have always served HEMP well. That's why we came to think of them as "the other half of mentoring."

Earlier in our history, we successfully partnered with the Kauffman Foundation for programs. They would pay to bring world-class speakers to Kansas City; we would be invited to attend, often at no charge. Occasionally, we had the same arrangement with the UMKC Bloch School of Management and others.

Now, as we have matured, we have shifted responsibility for choosing topics and presenters to the program chair and committee. Although quality was usually high because HEMPers were well-connected, we began to hear that the randomness was confusing and sometimes didn't meet basic needs.

The solution made great sense. At program chair Bill Hartnett's direction, the Program Committee established "content buckets" typical of second-stage businesses and challenged its members to ensure the yearly schedule of programs hit topics like marketing, human resources, operations, finance, and selling. No longer were we just chasing random speakers who presented well. There was now a rhythm to what we talked about, and the committee's task instead became finding the best and most timely presenters for the topics that mattered.

Three presentations I particularly encourage are embezzlement, hiring and firing, and selling. Embezzlement held special meaning because we'd had a participant go out of business after a trusted, family-friend bookkeeper stole $1 million from his company. We wanted to prevent a repeat of that disaster. We started our embezzlement program with me saying, "One of you in this room is most likely a victim of embezzlement as we speak." Shirley said I may have scared our participants, but I replied, "Good. That is what I wanted to do."

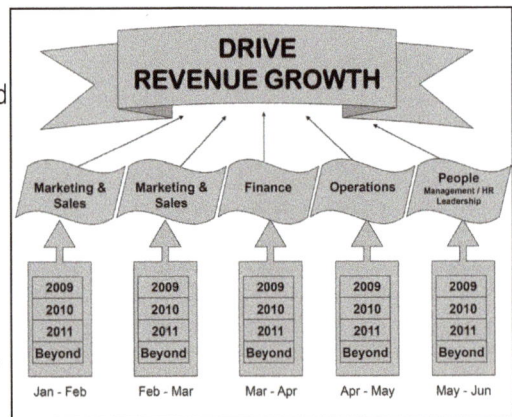

HEMP Program Committee chart.

As soon as program topics were in place, participants clearly understood what they would learn. It was a win.

> ## Three presentations I particularly encourage are embezzlement, hiring and firing, and selling.

When Deborah Young was our president, she also created a 360-degree feedback program for Mentees, complete with excellent feedback from an experienced coach. This assessment is available during the Mentees' first year and again the third year of participation so they can compare results.

She also started a goal-setting program for all new Mentee-Mentor pairs to attend within the first sixty days of the new program year. This program helps establish communication about priorities and quickly gets our new teams in motion.

Another great benefit for our Mentees is a highly informative financial review completed by our Finance Committee in their first year. Initially, these were optional, but as one Mentor observed, "Those who need them the most seem slowest to sign up." The results of these reviews are done with both the Mentee and their Mentor so they can discuss collectively those areas that need attention and develop a plan of action.

We have an annual HEMP retreat for all participants and their guests. This is a full-day event complete with a prominent keynote speaker, several breakout educational workshops, a graduation ceremony, and a celebratory dinner. Featured keynote speakers have included noted vulnerability researcher and author Brené Brown, Apple cofounder Steve Wozniak, Whole Foods Market CEO and co-founder John Mackey, Kansas City Royals president Dayton Moore, QuikTrip chairman and CEO Chet Cadieux, and many more. They share their stories and challenges with our participants in an open and vulnerable way. Our HEMPers are inspired and grateful for this access to entrepreneurs who have passionately started a business and fought their way to a high level of success. HEMPers always look forward to these special features offered at every retreat:

Kansas City Royals president, Dayton Moore, speaking at a HEMP retreat.

- Goodie bags with gifts from our participants such as pens, gift cards and fun tchotchkes
- An updated Resource Guide with contact information for all our wonderful people
- Ample networking time throughout the day
- Chair massages to unwind and relax
- Our signature "Kool-Aid" (The late Barney Karbank, lovingly called HEMP a "cult" because of the unique bonds that develop between participants. We joke about "drinking the Kool-Aid" so we offer our favorite green smoothies as representation of this.)

Bill Hartnett

When Bill Hartnett was our president, we wanted to do something special in the spirit of keeping HEMP fun and to celebrate our twentieth year. He was a key leader during this amazing event that took our annual retreat to the next level. Steve Wozniak was our keynote speaker, and we opened access to paid tickets for the local community. In addition, three important awards were created to give recognition to individuals who have shown a devoted commitment to growing business in Kansas City: Lifetime Achievement in Entrepreneurial Mentoring, Corporate Mentor of the Year, and Entrepreneurial Mentor of the Year.

Moderator Mike Lundgren interviews Apple co-founder Steve Wozniak during HEMP's 20th anniversary event.

Bill and Kerry Hartnett with Steve Wozniak.

Resources for the Fellows

Back in 2004, a committee of HEMPers had formalized the new group they chose to call Fellows. These were participants who had graduated as Mentees and wanted to remain in the program. Fellows pay a reduced annual fee and are welcome to all HEMP events and resources.

Since its formation, this group has become an integral part of HEMP. Besides financial support for the organization, Fellows have provided peer mentoring, connections, and ongoing networking. They have made themselves available both with time and financial advice when they are needed, oftentimes chairing and/or participating in our committees. They have especially helped with what we call forum groups, small gatherings of business peers who help and hold one another accountable for growth initiatives and problem solving.

More focus on this invaluable group was a good investment! We started with a Fellows' happy hour (Thirsty Thursdays) that met quarterly to provide an opportunity for the connections that gave them an identity. Later, we would add a breakfast club and other meeting opportunities to socialize, learn, and give. Like the Mentees, members of this peer group of entrepreneurs face similar challenges and experiences. This coordinated time together reminds them of the valuable resources available to them in HEMP—resources who already practice the Spirits of The Big Guy (page 116).

The HEMP Class of 2014 celebrating their graduation and induction into the Fellows.

HEMP Fellows Jim Weir, Kevin Tubbesing and Austin Bickford at a Fellows' Thirsty Thursday.

Settling Funding Questions

The whole question of funding HEMP first raised its ugly head earlier than we expected as part of a discussion of whether to institute program-length expectations for Mentees. Finances and program length don't appear to be related, but they are. We had begun as an organization with a couple of funding sources: The Shirley and Barnett C. Helzberg, Jr. Foundation and a three-year generous start-up grant from the Kauffman Foundation.

If we'd had one-year expectations for Mentees, our organizational size would be net zero annually. We would gain twenty Mentees and, at year's end, lose twenty. But that wasn't how we worked. Mentees stayed onboard if the relationship was working, so each year we would add new Mentees but lose only a handful. The same was true for Mentors. Even those currently unassigned to a Mentee offered to stay around as a resource as needed. We were finding that once people came to us, they didn't want to leave. Apparently, there was such a thing as HEMP addiction!

One Mentor said, "To me, this isn't so much a social club as an insurance policy. The premium payment for my policy is in how I help you. But the day is going to come when I need help; that's the nature of business. And this outfit is full of smart people—that's what comes from having it be so damn hard to get in! When I'm struggling, I know some people will jump in to help."

This was an excellent reassurance that the resources we offered were useful. The problem was if people stayed on and on, and we kept supporting them to the same degree, we would need to add additional team members and programming options to accommodate the increased size. It was clear these additions would cost money. Where would it be generated?

We'd had the privilege from the start to enjoy sponsorship that didn't take time to recruit. We didn't want to fill the board with people who had connections or finances to bankroll us but cared little about the organization. Additionally, we wanted HEMPers to have the freedom to give full focus to the mission of HEMP without the distraction of continual fundraising.

As a jump start, we soon instituted a reasonable solution of adding fees for Mentees. As we began to formalize the roles and resources to Fellows, we added a yearly participation fee for this group, too. Neither of these changes got pushback. It seemed clear to participants by then that the resources they were receiving in mentoring, networking, and community were worth underwriting.

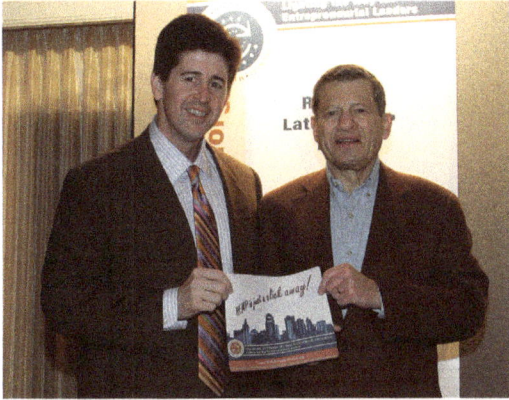

Barnett C. Helzberg, Jr. thanking Rick Krska for his contribution, which launched HEMP's first professional website.

Although all our participants were contributing to our finances through dues, we still needed more income. Some sources appeared naturally. HEMPers enjoyed the Lunch with The Big Guy experience, and some asked to host the meeting at their places of business with an offer to pick up the tab. When we hit special growth-generated needs, like the creation of a first-class website, Rick Krska, a participant with a particular interest in this area, offered underwriting for the project. Others gave time and expertise to its development as in-kind gifts. This experience of unsolicited donations coming to help underwrite the website was pivotal in our thinking about money. HEMPers were ready to help and wanted to give back.

We got bolder and dabbled in more formal fundraising techniques, such as an annual golf tournament, silent auctions as part of special celebrations, and requests for donations to mark playful "anniversaries" like my eighty-fifth birthday. We created large Mentee recruiting ads for the local newspaper featuring photos of Mentees who pay a fee to participate. The Mentee classes also got involved and began presenting either a donation or gift to HEMP in celebration of their graduation from their formal three-year mentoring experience.

These initiatives weren't part of some long-range strategic funding plan. As was our way, we were pretty much making it up as we went along with our hallmark low-risk experiments. By 2013, we moved to a once-a-year fundraising event. This extra fundraising underwrites special projects, while the fees paid by Mentees and Fellows carry HEMP's operating expenses. We have been careful to expand team members based on quality not quantity, so operating within our budget is workable.

66 Quality not quantity. 99

This funding question may come up again as organizational needs change, but for now, we're still free to give time, energy, and full attention to getting it right for Mentees and Mentors. Nothing could be better.

Marketing HEMP Better

If we had an ongoing question in HEMP, it was how to bring new Mentees into the program. By second stage, entrepreneurs have learned to look before they jump and hold at arm's length the testimonials that come their way. Plus, in our case, to go from a casual interest in HEMP to completing a very demanding application process is a giant leap. The procedure involves a $150 application fee, a background check, a DiSC evaluation, providing references, taking an online course about expectations, and, of course, the actual application.

We had tried many ways to let applicants know what HEMP had to offer. After all, what's the use of great Mentors if there aren't ready Mentees open to their help?

We had begun to talk with business leaders who might be natural marketing partners. Bankers, attorneys, and investment professionals know second-stage entrepreneurs they might refer to HEMP. These referrals could benefit them, too, because as these entrepreneurs grow their businesses through mentoring, they also increase in value as clients. Everybody wins. Also, during this "getting better" stage, we came upon an idea that has worked well: the introductory HEMP Lunch and Learn.

It sounds almost too simple. Current HEMPers invite others they think might be interested in becoming Mentees or Mentors to a luncheon at Barnett's Basement. It's just lunch—no commitment other than that. Then after introductions and some comfort-building socialization, we follow with a program explaining HEMP's benefits and costs, complete with stories from Mentors and Mentees who have seen it be useful. They see a video of our origin story and results and leave with an invite to consider participating. If they sign up immediately, they receive a discount on our fee.

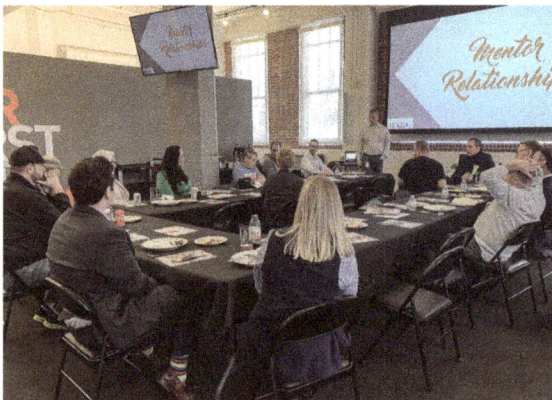

A group of Lunch and Learn attendees listening to Barnett C. Helzberg, Jr. speak about his experience.

HEMP Fellow Danielle Debbrecht (middle) talking with Lunch and Learn participants.

We learned this low-risk yet personal exposure to HEMP via the experiences of satisfied participants was the key we'd been seeking. They would hear stories from businesspeople they recognized, told with vulnerability, ease, and humor. They would see the warm and inclusive HEMP relationships alive within the room and become acquainted with such HEMP-specific phrases as "Put your worst foot forward."

It offered an excellent opportunity to admit to and "sell" the very high commitment asked of those applying. Lunch and Learn speaker Robin Royals, a Kansas City consultant and HEMP Mentor, colorfully described his amazement at the application process that followed an invitation to be a Mentor. "They were asking me to volunteer my time," he said, shaking his head, "then went right on to insist I apply, then be interviewed before I'd be accepted. What was it about 'volunteer' they didn't understand?" He let attendees know he felt their pain as they went through the application process, but he assured them their acceptance would mean participation in a select, high-quality, highly committed group of entrepreneurial peers. It was worth the effort of applying to access a vetted advisor who came with a completely unbiased view and no interest in them except contributing to their success.

These Lunch and Learn events seem to bridge the gap between casual interest and looking seriously at the application process. It is a step-by-step marketing approach, and it has fit our potential Mentee base well.

HEMP needed to continue to up its game. These changes made a big difference, but they also increased our determination to keep the quality of participants and resources trending steadily upward.

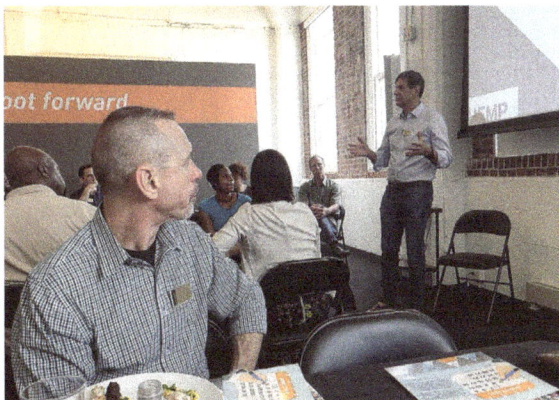

Lunch and Learn attendee listening to HEMP Mentor Gordon Harton share his story.

Attendees will always eat good food at a HEMP event, especially a Lunch and Learn!

Part 5: Designing HEMP's Future

(2018–2020)

HEMP group at an early Schmooze Fest.

CHAPTER 8

A Culture That Lasts

I got more serious about the future sustainability of HEMP as the result of a car accident. A tree jumped out and hit my car. I came out of the accident fine but getting to full recovery for a broken leg required time in a rehab facility. I'm telling you, if you need to get a little more reflective, there's nothing like being stuck in a medical setting to do it.

Twenty years earlier, when we switched from a loose steering-committee structure to a governance board, my joke-rationale for handing off the president's role started with, "When I go to my reward . . . "so, for years I'd been throwing out the reality that I wouldn't always be here as a way to wonder aloud what we were building for the future.

Scott King

I have always been more lucky than smart, and about that time, a culture-development company presented at a HEMP program on the need to define, describe, and develop a company culture. Until then I thought "culture" was pretty much like air: We knew it was necessary but invisible, so it was easy to take it for granted. It was something to enjoy and use but not something that might need attention. If I had defined HEMP's culture, I would have talked more about what we did—mentoring, community building—than about the unique ways we went about it. Those culture folks emphasized culture as a driver. Particular programs and policies could shift with the times, but culture, if it were intentional, would last.

HEMP president Scott King quickly linked what he was hearing about culture to our conversations about HEMP's future from when I was hospitalized. Scott talked with the presenters about working with HEMP to clarify and help ensure a culture we loved would remain. He was smart enough to reframe the idea this way: to establish a "steady drumbeat" for HEMP's cultural heart.

Management genius Peter Drucker once said, "Culture eats strategy for breakfast." I think that quote has staying power because it's counterintuitive to some who see business as systems and processes, checks and balances, and bylaws. Culture sounds soft and mushy. It's harder to measure than profitability and more challenging to capture than a paid-time-off policy. We had ignored giving culture our attention but couldn't ignore its impact. Scott helped us see that HEMP hadn't thrived for nearly a quarter century because we had always had the smartest strategies. We hadn't. Nor was it because we always knew what we were doing. We didn't. We had thrived because at the heart of HEMP was a foundation for doing the work we did. That foundation, thanks to the good people devoted to it, had only strengthened through the years. They loved it, reinforced it, and attracted more like themselves to the organization.

As former HEMP president Bill Hartnett said, "Culture becomes a pervasive juggernaut of what the group is. And culture's not by accident. It can be by accident, but you don't get a healthy, perpetuating culture by accident."

So, we went to work trying to define what the building blocks of this elusive but critical foundation were. We formed a culture team that asked question after question, rephrasing, challenging, distilling, poking hard to find out what mattered most in making us what we are. In the end, we settled on four core values and began floating them to the rest of the organization for feedback. Here's where we landed.

Four Core Values = Spirits of The Big Guy

The term values applied to the heart of business never resonated with me. Out of respect for my reluctance, the team labeled these HEMP's Spirits of The Big Guy. I think they were poking fun at me, but they tell me it's because they want to further my legacy. Hence, HEMP's Spirits of The Big Guy was the name of our core values.

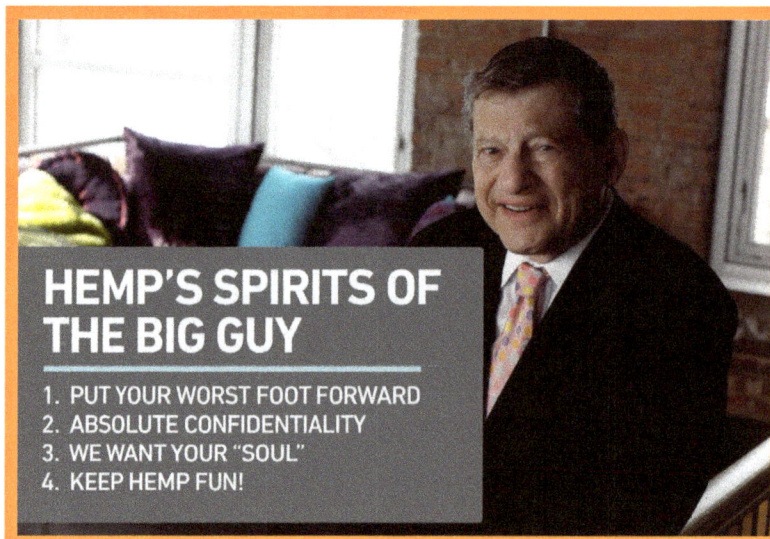

HEMP'S SPIRITS OF THE BIG GUY

1. PUT YOUR WORST FOOT FORWARD
2. ABSOLUTE CONFIDENTIALITY
3. WE WANT YOUR "SOUL"
4. KEEP HEMP FUN!

1. Put Your Worst Foot Forward

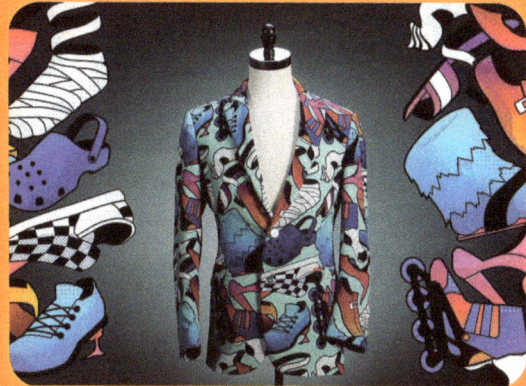

A high bar was set for us on the day that our founders met in the infamous basement for the first time. It happened when real estate mogul Barney Karbank led his introduction not with his astounding business success but rather with the story of a kid with leg braces struggling to keep up with the other boys.

We began to understand we needed to give this idea of what story to tell more attention when one of our Mentors told us his mentee's business was collapsing. The Mentor was surprised because his Mentee worked hard to keep the reports positive, but the issues they discussed were superficial. "We would have all pulled together and helped her make it work," the Mentor said, shaking his head. "I never knew."

> **Seeing his distress, I wrote in a newsletter article, "Your HEMP Mentor is a resource for bad days to help you look for alternatives and solve problems. The Mentor can't be the dentist who asks, 'What hurts?' to which the patient replies, 'You're the dentist, you tell me.' To get the most out of your mentoring experience, spend your time on problems, not triumphs! Good Mentees Put Your Worst Foot Forward!"**

We began to circulate stories that let Mentors know vulnerability was as critical for them as it was for the Mentees. This note I received from one of our Mentees illustrates that need:

I have owned my own business for almost fourteen years. In all that time, I never had a moment where I wasn't eager to face the challenges that greet entrepreneurs each day. Well, I faced that moment a few weeks ago. I could not get back on the horse. I knew my staff was waiting for me at the office. There were calls to return and materials to get out. But I just couldn't find the energy to do it, so what's a Mentee to do?

I called my Mentor. Somehow, I knew that her voice was the only one I was going to listen to at that moment. I told her she'd probably think I was nuts, but that I couldn't get motivated to go into the office.

Her response was, "You know, that happened to me just last week, and here's what I did. . . ." When I needed it most, she gave me a leg up. This program isn't just about getting advice on writing business plans, crunching numbers, or business strategies. It's [also] about knowing that there's someone out there that cares enough to catch you when you fall. All you need is the courage to ask.

This Mentee was right about asking, but just as important, his Mentor had to be willing to say, "That happened to me . . . ," and put *her* worst foot forward. The saying stuck. Our participants value a confidential safe place to share their concerns that they can't necessarily share anywhere else. "It's lonely at the top" is an accurate saying, and at HEMP we want to alleviate some of that pressure. We emphasize this so much that if you visit our event space in the Crossroads, you'll see Put Your Worst Foot Forward painted in two-foot-high letters on the wall and artfully plastered on HEMP T-shirts.

How we Put Our Worst Foot Forward:

🍁 Coach Mentors to intentionally include their lessons from failures, not just successes.

🍁 In selection interviews, be sure to ask about and listen to the disclosure of struggles and failures to help determine if the interviewee is a fit.

🍁 At HEMP's yearly State of HEMP gathering, share the organization's financials and remind participants we're doing this to maintain openness with them.

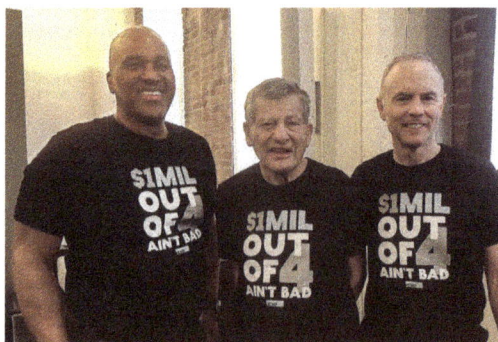

Mentors Robin Royals, Barnett C. Helzberg, Jr. and Dave Perky celebrating HEMP's restricted reserve fund hitting $1 million of its $4 million goal.

2. Absolute Confidentiality

This was a given from Day One. The Mentors were businesspeople and knew by experience—and some scars—how careful the leader must be in disclosing anything. One casual remark from an unsuspecting listener floats to a critical person, and for reasons nobody could foresee, all hell breaks loose. That poker instruction to keep your cards close to your chest is a bylaw for Mentees and Mentors. However, it can hinder mentoring because, without disclosure, Mentors may be helping with the wrong—and nonexistent—problems. That can be worse than no help at all.

HEMPers "keeping their cards close to their chest" at a Casino Night.

We agreed from the start that absolute confidentiality had to be a given every day this organization functioned. Mentees needed to know what they disclosed would go nowhere without their permission. This must be true not only in the Mentor-Mentee relationship but also in our peer forums, Lunch with The Big Guy conversations, social hours during our retreats—all of it!

In twenty-five years, we've never had to ask a Mentor or Mentee to leave the organization for breaking confidentiality. If such a breach occurred, dismissal would follow immediately. It's nonnegotiable.

This value was the easiest of the four to define. What happens at HEMP, stays at HEMP!

How we ensure Absolute Confidentiality:

🌿 On Mentee selection site visits, we prepare a separate notebook section for each candidate with a report about the leader and his or her business, and take only the interviewee's information to the conversation. That way, there's less chance anyone knows who else is being considered. These notebooks get shredded right after the site-visit day—no taking them home. Plus, when we stop for lunch on site-visit days, we make sure the restaurant gives us a private room, so our evaluations happen behind closed doors. (I razz Christina on every visit when we are about to go in and ask if we can bring our notebooks. Everyone says "NO!" in unison.)

🌿 As Mentees proceed through the selection process, we ask them to submit financials through a secure system to ensure that only the intended recipients see them.

🌿 Every accepted Mentee and Mentor sign a confidentiality statement.

🌿 Our Resource Guide has a confidentiality statement and only HEMP participants have access to those resources.

3. We Want Your "Soul"

Let's be clear from the outset: I'm the one who insisted we use the word *soul*.

"But that word has religious connotations," HEMP participants protested. I knew that, but I wanted to overemphasize a point that can't be overemphasized—that of commitment.

A couple of decades with HEMP convinced us of this: those who gain most from HEMP are those who show up, who meet with their Mentors, who come to events, and who are willing to help and willing to be helped. For a busy, stretched, stressed entrepreneur whose business is consuming, those choices don't come easily.

We had examples of some who wasted their time and the time of the highly skilled business leaders who had committed to help them. They blew a spot that might have gone to another who would have profited from participation.

We generated the idea of a "soul" commitment by accident. When we would do site visits to help select applicants for interviews as potential mentees, I was usually last in the lineup of questioners. I would go after the interviewee. "What are you involved in?" I would probe. Then, "With all those commitments, how are you going to have time for HEMP? Besides mentoring, we expect you to attend 75 percent of the events." Then I would move to my big finish. "We're not a cult," I would conclude in as serious a voice as I could muster, "but we want your soul!" A catchphrase was born.

When talking about our core values, we floated the idea of this *soul* language and listened to the pushback. There was plenty from the Board, who spent a big part of a one-day retreat wrangling over it. However, when we presented the idea to the participants, we got no feedback—positive or negative—at all. It seemed obvious to our participants, and they thought this was already a core value!

Barnett C. Helzberg, Jr. and Mentor Lirel Holt dancing to "Soul Man" at State of HEMP.

In the end, the very fact that it was a loaded word almost gave it more power. If we had substituted the word *commitment*, which is what we meant, of course, it wouldn't have generated the same conversation about what we expected.

Using the word *soul* also gave us a platform to remind participants of what integrity meant to us. We pointed to integrity in business dealings and in being a part of HEMP. Integrity is to give and get but not to use. If you were manipulative, it's easy to see what a gold mine the HEMP community might become. You would see buyers for your products or recommenders for your company or donors for your nonprofit. That's not HEMP. HEMP had to be a safe place for successful entrepreneurs to seek help and to offer support without worrying about being manipulated by an asker with hidden, self-serving motives.

So yes, we wanted your soul, by which we meant your all-in involvement. Others were already giving it. By pledging your commitment, you were joining a community ready to commit to you in return.

How we find the right people (We Want Your "Soul"):

🌿 Keep the process of applying to HEMP as stringent as it needs to be, not to create unnecessary elitist hoops to jump through but to help communicate the message of commitment. If there isn't enough time and interest to complete the application, there won't be enough time to make something of the HEMP experience.

🌿 We are a participant-driven organization and we get better each year because of HEMPers' ideas and suggestions. We continue to welome and act on feedback so our participants want to invest their time in HEMP.

Lirel Holt and Brent Niemuth performing "Soul Man."

4. Keep HEMP Fun!

If you put together the combined balance sheets, visibility, and influence of the group attending HEMP events, you would have a high-powered and damned serious crowd. They carry responsibility for large numbers of lives and livelihoods and do not for a moment take it lightly.

What helps pry us open to one another and learning is having fun together. Lots and lots of laughing and goofiness go on that no book on business behavior would recommend.

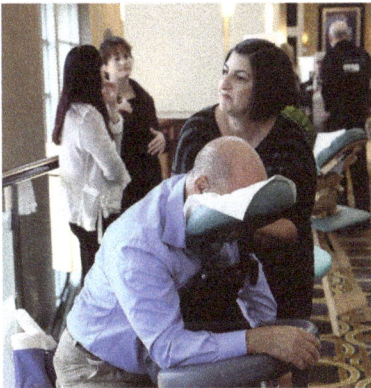

A HEMPer relaxing with a chair massage at a HEMP event.

Some of the fun is low-key and not too surprising, like offering chair massages at the annual retreat or turning our yearly HEMP celebration into a casino night. But others are more purposely off-the-wall, such as our first day in our new Crossroads office when we baked brownies with green sprinkles—aka HEMP brownies—and passed them out to the other tenants in the building. There's also the sign on our office door that reads "HEMP. Open For Business!" Then, too, I show up at events in my specially designed and tailored HEMP business suit made of marijuana leaf–printed fabric. And everyone loves the hilarious "rock-video" adaptations our audiovisual company, owned by HEMP supporter and Fellow Austin Bickford, creates to celebrate each of the Mentees on graduation day.

We also assign each new Mentee class the task of creating a skit for its first retreat. (This came about by telling the 2014 class of Mentees that the skit was a HEMP tradition. No tradition existed, of course, but with that first performance a tradition was born!) Often these skits poke fun at me, like the drama that involved my arrest for selling hemp (HEMP!), being dragged into court, then both defended and prosecuted by Mentee "attorneys." Due to my inept lawyer, I was to end up in the Graybar Hotel, pleading for the proverbial cake with a file baked inside.

The HEMP Class of 2017 performing their class skit.

Does all of this sound a little ridiculous for folks whose businesses are generating at least a million dollars a year? Maybe. But we found that if we could quickly laugh together, we could much more quickly come to one another with the things that keep us up at night. And that, of course, was the goal.

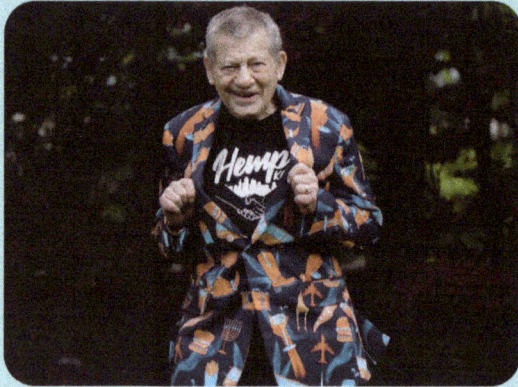

Life as an entrepreneur is tough and pressured and lonely. Laughter energizes and sometimes sustains us. And it had to be part of HEMP for the duration.

How we Keep HEMP Fun!:

🌿 Give meeting spaces and refreshments a personal touch of fun. Stock up on participants' favorite beverages and set up tables to generate easy mixing. Add "nonessential" playful touches like champagne at celebration meetings.

🌿 In Mentee selection interviews, ask unexpected questions that reveal a penchant for goofiness, like "Who is your favorite cartoon character and why?"

🌿 We play up the HEMP name in many ways, such as hosting events on 4/20 or wearing marijuana leaf clothing.

🌿 We include fun and playful aspects at every event, whether it be a theme night or a silly game.

Christina Dreiling and Maggie Johnson serving champagne at State of HEMP.

These actions got us going, and the team set up the goal of a quarterly review to assess what we had done to embed HEMP's Spirits of The Big Guy through reminder and application.

Culture Embedding

We had *defined* our four spirits, or core values. The next step was to *declare* them to participants through repetition, T-shirts, notebook covers, and the rest. But how could we ensure HEMP would continue to *demonstrate* these core values? We settled on the most obvious solution, the same one we would use for instilling and measuring our effectiveness at any initiative. We would make ourselves accountable. We started by looking at current and future behaviors that would teach or remind us of these values. Here are just a few examples of how we keep each core value at full power.

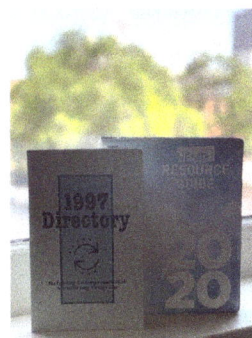

Making Sure the Spirits Suited Us

Mindy Corporon and Dr. Michelle Robin hug Barnett C. Helzberg, Jr. (wearing his Lilly Pulitzer jacket) at Schmooze Fest 2014.

As a final, funny, quasi-mocking creation to say "spirits matter," Fellow Austin Bickford and other HEMPers had designed and tailored four sports jackets for me. Each was cut from a fabric patterned to one of the four spirits.

HEMPers came to this decision naturally. For years, I would often show up at meetings in a sports coat that always got attention. Lilly Pulitzer designed highly patterned, gorgeous clothes for such socially prominent figures as Jacqueline Kennedy and the Rockefeller and Vanderbilt families. When she came up with a man's jacket made from a noisy, colorful pink-and-blue paisley fabric, I had found my choice. I love the unexpected, but as the constant social companion of the beautiful and elegant Shirley Helzberg, anything that edges toward goofiness has to be restrained. But come on, this was a Lilly Pulitzer—even if I did find it at a thrift store for sixty dollars! So that jacket became a best friend, and even more so when once on a HEMP field trip in Las Vegas, a silly (and probably a little drunk) gaggle of young women at a bachelorette party insisted on photos with the old guy in the goofy jacket. The coat became iconic.

That's why when Christina saw an online ad for a suit made from a hemp-emblazoned fabric, she invested all of $150 on the hemp-leaf jacket, slacks, tie, and fanny pack. This led to hemp-adorned shirts and other wearables, so a "brand" was born.

You might ask, a fanny pack? I always wear a fanny pack. I like to tell everyone it's to carry my diabetes supplies, but it's my go-to accessory for all necessities—phone, peanuts, mustard packets, keys, my favorite fountain pens. My fanny packs have become a family heirloom. When I wear out the zippers and must get a new pack, you can find the used ones in my grandkids' playroom. Pee-Paw's fanny packs make great playthings.

HEMP Fellow Brandy McCombs points out Barnett C. Helzberg, Jr.'s fanny pack.

Therefore, it seemed logical to HEMPers that each spirit of the organization should have a jacket of its own, so Christina had four jackets made up for me to that end. It was culture communication through wardrobing.

Absolute Confidentiality came through clearly in a design created from an actual article about HEMP, with words redacted all over it. *Put Your Worst Foot Forward* was pictured, as you likely guessed, as a collection of all sorts of strange footwear.

We Want Your "Soul" included pictures of the Kool-Aid Man. (This referenced the cult slogan about "drinking the Kool-Aid." We had concocted a special hemp-green drink for meetings, but nothing poisonous ever evolved.) There were sharks as a reminder that HEMP participants are the sharks of business in Kansas City, gobbling up the competition. And there was an hourglass, clock, and briefcase to represent the giving of time. It's business time, after all. The Grim Reaper was there, too—as in, it's all or nothing in this community!

Not surprisingly, our favorite jacket was the one picturing *Keep HEMP Fun!* It started with pictures of suitcases and planes, reminiscent of HEMP trips marked by as much fun as business acumen. A bus (the Mentee site visits) and dice (Las Vegas), cowboy boots (Austin, TX), and a Viking helmet (Iceland) appeared as reminders of experiences on our shared travels. There were menorahs scattered here and there, lest anyone forget my penchant for terrible Jewish jokes, along with a burger and fries (eating together) and martini glasses (celebrations).

But the best part was the rubber chicken. Remember the rubber chicken that I presented to Ray Pitman and that then called me at random, inconvenient times?

HEMPers know how to communicate culture! We wear our creativity with pride.

The Feeling of HEMP

We've created our four core values, HEMP's Spirits of The Big Guy, but the whole story of HEMP includes many small traditions adapted over time and carefully and thoughtfully managed by Christina and her team. These traditions evoke positive emotions in HEMPers.

Walt Rychlewski ringing the cowbell.

Cowbell

At all of our events, we allow time for our participants to network with one another. Getting the meeting started, according to Christina, is like "herding cats." We ring a cowbell to get everyone's attention and signal when it is time to find a seat. We have expanded this tradition to include a small cowbell with the HEMP logo and their name engraved as part of our welcome gift to new Mentors. Mentors also receive a tiny cowbell with our logo each time they have a Mentee graduate. We give a golden cowbell with his or her name engraved to each Mentee graduate as well. It may seem strange to some, but you will see many golden cowbells proudly displayed in entrepreneurs' offices throughout the Kansas City area.

Peanuts

As a small token of appreciation for our participants' time and service at our meetings, we like to share some simple yet carefully selected snacks with them. One of my favorites is peanuts. Not only are these peanuts at our meetings, but we also send them to our participants in a modest show of gratitude for going a step above on our behalf. We always include a handwritten note!

Our favorite peanuts

HEMP "Kool-Aid" green smoothies

Green smoothies

It was the late Barney Karbank who lovingly called HEMP a "cult" because of the unique bonds that develop among the participants. HEMPers often joke about "drinking the Kool-Aid," so today we offer our favorite green smoothies as a representation of the infamous HEMP Kool-Aid. Thank you to HEMP Fellow Michelle Robin for introducing us all to this great recipe.

HEMPers have tremendous demands on their time. We have worked hard not only to create an intellectual reason to continue active participation but also to create an emotional connection that evokes feelings of welcome, acceptance, comfort, safety, gratitude, and love.

These traditions are a part of the known elements HEMP participants can expect. Like everything else, we will continue to listen for more favorites and comforts to add to our list.

One participant said it best: "I walk into Barnett's Basement and I can feel my shoulders relax and a smile cross my face. I am energized and excited to talk to my peers I haven't seen in a while. I know I am going to learn something today."

The Pandemic as a Test

When the COVID-19 pandemic spread worldwide in 2020, HEMP was not immune. Meetings instantly became virtual without time for preparation. We serve growing businesses, some of the very companies that quarantines and stay-at-home orders sucker punched economically.

When I understood the implications of what was coming, I told our participants that Winston Churchill's words when England was at a point of desperation were echoing in my head. "This may be our finest hour!" And at this writing, I would say the HEMP community is rising to my prediction within our shared challenge.

First came a reinvention of events. Like many organizations, we moved swiftly to online meetings. Zoom is well known now, but it wasn't used regularly or comfortably before COVID.The HEMP team quickly created ways to show our spirit, even with this limitation.

The monthly Lunch with The Big Guy problem-solving conversations quickly shifted online, as they were now more important than ever as

| LETTER TO THE EDITOR |

Barnett Helzberg keeps Mr. K's spirit alive

I was a junior at Blue Valley North High School when Ewing Kauffman passed away, and I never had a chance to meet him. But 17 years later, as an entrepreneur with a growing business, I can still feel Mr. K's impact on his beloved hometown.

This is in no small part due to one man, Barnett Helzberg Jr. -- who led Helzberg Diamonds' growth from 15 stores to more than 140 stores in 23 states before he sold the company, started by his grandfather, in 1995. That same year, inspired by his long mentoring relationship with Mr. K and a sincere desire to "pay it forward," Barnett created the Helzberg Entrepreneurship Mentoring Program. HEMP pairs successful entrepreneur mentors with less-experienced entrepreneur mentees. *Fast Company* cited HEMP recently as one reason "Why You Should Start a Company in Kansas City."

Barnett's warmth, good humor and humility make him one of the most endearing people I have met. If you listen to him long enough, you will find that underneath his charismatic and self-deprecating nature, he is a shrewd businessman, smart enough to learn from mistakes and kind enough to share his wisdom to empower others.

His genuine care for people and generosity of spirit drives HEMP and cements the special bond that its members have with one another. On Nov. 9, I was reminded of this as I watched the latest class of HEMP mentees graduate. Each entrepreneur recounted how he or she overcame significant business and personal challenges thanks to the relationships they established in HEMP.

I am honored and continually proud to be associated with these amazing entrepreneurs. As a member of the strategic planning committee charting the transition of effective leadership from Barnett and his longtime friends to those who have risen through the program, I have never been more excited for HEMP's future.

Barnett is the torchbearer of Mr. K's entrepreneurial legacy. Through HEMP, he has touched the lives of hundreds who undoubtedly will touch the lives of thousands more. If we learn from the example he continues to set, I am confident Kansas City will be a great place to start a company for generations to come.

Neal Sharma
CEO, Digital Evolution Group LLC

A news article written by HEMP Fellow Neal Sharma.

A virtual HEMP meeting being held over Zoom.

participants struggled toward new solutions. Based on the suggestion of HEMP president Tracy Lockton, the team members arranged lunch delivery from the top caterer in Kansas City to the home of every participant. The Mentors' happy hour went online, too, with a gift bag of wine, beer, and cocktail ingredients dropped off at each Mentor's door so the "social" part of a social hour could go on.

Changes weren't only logistical or social. The Mentors' happy-hour conversation focused on how each of their Mentees were doing in the crisis and how we could share resources to support them. A reminder to include the Fellows resulted in current Mentors volunteering to make check-in calls to see who might need help.

The Board and team members started an aggressive and frequent email information-sharing support system with small-business relief program contacts, Centers for Disease Control and Prevention updates, crisis leadership and communication coaching, and self-care encouragement. Specialized Mentors offered not only deep dives into the financials of anyone needing help but also to work with any participant navigating a specific problem.

Zoom meetings became stale quickly so we tried to spice them up with new and different ideas, such as this costume contest.

Also born during this 2020 pandemic was President-elect Tracy Lockton's idea for a Master Mentee Program. This program for Fellows is a one-year partnership between a Fellow and a new Mentor. The initial idea was that this would be a special time of need when our participants are working to survive and retool to meet the changing demands of the new era. What we quickly learned was that there is an ongoing need for this program beyond 2020 because our HEMPers are in a constant state of change and growth. Listening to the needs of our participants wins again.

Tracy Lockton

In response to HEMP's outreach, a Mentee wrote the following:

Being a small business owner in the thick of COVID-19 is extra stressful. Hard questions around how to deal with the sudden derailment of nearly everything will shake the most seasoned entrepreneur. Information is flowing so fast and from so many directions that it is consuming all hours of the day.

One of the few bright spots has been HEMP. It has come crashing through the darkness to shine a light on information that truly matters to a small business owner. When COVID-19 started to impact the Kansas City area, the team was on top of it. They were immediately sifting through the sea of information and filtering out what was relevant for HEMPers. Soon after, the entire HEMP organization started banding together and providing resources to help answer scary questions like, What is my worst-case scenario? Should I start sending people home? If I don't, am I liable? Should I start applying for small business loans now? What should I be telling my people?

Confronting questions like these with a team of trusted professionals and confidants is how businesses survive devastating times like this. The requirements of absolute confidentiality and worst foot forward allow participants to speak their minds and work toward real solutions to make their business better.

HEMP participants also received help with business-improvement ideas. One Mentor told me his conversations during the pandemic included asking, "What are you looking at that is going to help you in the future?" In response, one Mentee changed his supplier model so that China was no longer his only source. Another said, "I'm rethinking the organization now that everything is up in the air anyway." Future focus was work, not just putting out fires.

Snacks and beverages were delivered to each of these recipients' homes before the virtual happy hour.

It's the kind of community spirit HEMPers have come to expect, and they are both receiving and giving with grace.

I have to admit I was scared for our HEMPers. They continue to amaze me with their resilience, creativity, and drive. I was overwhelmed to hear at our online meetings that our HEMPers were actually growing and expanding. Of course, that was not happening without many sleepless nights, countless hours of thought, and hopefully conversations with fellow HEMPers.

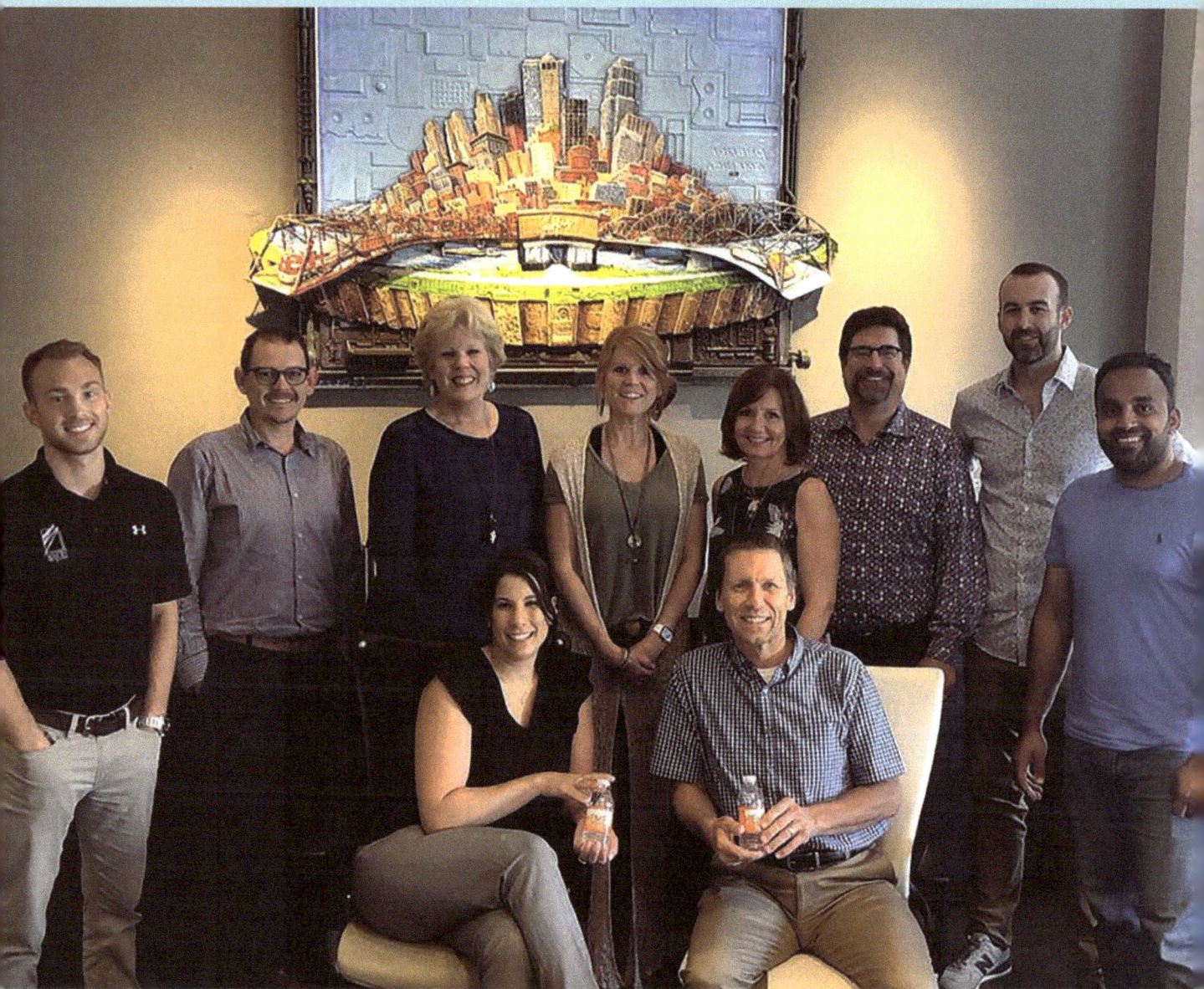

The incoming Class of 2018 Happy Hour where we surprise them with the news they'll be presenting a skit during the HEMP retreat dinner.

CHAPTER 9

To All That's Ahead

You know where we've come from and how we got where we are here in year twenty-five. Now, here's what we know for sure about HEMP's future:

1. It's going to be lively.
2. It's going to involve change.
3. It's going to be built by strong, smart, brave, listening business leaders ready to grow, learn, improve, and invest themselves in the success of others.

I think you will agree with this projection when you hear a sampling of just three of the improvement ideas current participants have generated.

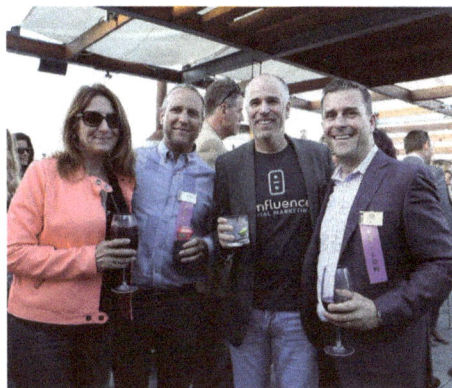

Laura Lee Jones, Ron Hill, Dave Cacioppo, and Jon Schram raise a glass at Celebrate HEMP.

"I'd love for the movers and shakers in the Kansas City community to know about our mission and refer people to us. I've had business leaders tell me, 'I've discovered you guys do great work; I just didn't know you were here.' I'd love to see HEMP as a regular, go-to part of discussions about resources when the Chambers of Commerce or other visible entities talk about organizations making a difference."

"The pandemic is going to change the business landscape of America and the world dramatically. What resources do we need to create right now to help HEMPers who have lost their companies? And to help others pivot quickly to succeed in the new world?"

And a personal favorite: *"Fun is what keeps me coming back to HEMP. Being an entrepreneur is hard, hard work. We've got to keep this part of our spirit alive and well. How about a board position called Champion of Fun?"*

Entrepreneurs are, by their very nature, not maintainers. They shift and move and change and grow things, so an organization made up of them must do the same. Indeed, they'll see to it!

We're anticipating that as HEMPers make decisions about how to proceed, these three things will always be influential:

> 1. **They'll ask first, "Does it help Mentees?"**
> 2. **They'll proceed to fail small, succeed big by putting just one foot, not two, in to test the water's depth.**
> 3. **They'll watch the results both for the program's effectiveness and for whether it enhances or detracts from HEMP's Spirits of The Big Guy.**

HEMP won't lack for awareness of the business landscape or smart and timely ideas about ways both to respond to and create it. We hope this history and joy will make HEMP relevant for decades to come.

As we grow, change, and dream, we hope the spirit of HEMP, anchored in confidentiality, putting your worst foot forward, giving your soul, and doing it with a heavy dose of fun, will stay clear and true.

We hope the commitment to ever-improving experiences for Mentees and Mentors will grow only stronger.

The result of all this will be a joyful, committed, generous community of entrepreneurs who are seeking the best for one another and for Kansas City.

The future will be remarkable, and I can't wait.

HEMPingly yours,

TBG (The Big Guy)

HEMP Timeline

1995
HEMP is launched.

1997
First annual dinner is held at the Oakwood Country Club with special guest speaker Bob Rogers of the Kauffman Foundation.

Mentor-Mentee workshop is held featuring "Hiring and Retaining Quality" panel discussion.

First HEMP Resource Guide (participant directory) is published.

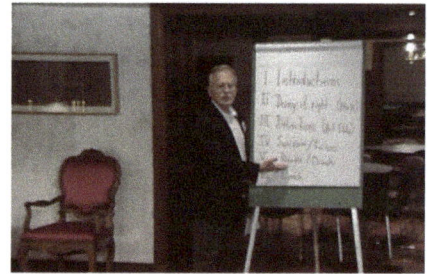

Harvey Thomas leading HEMP's first meeting in 1995.

1998
First HEMP annual retreat is held at The Elms in Excelsior Springs with special guest speakers Ted and Alice Cohn. Ted was notably one of Barnett's greatest mentors.

Mentor-Mentee workshop is held featuring "How You Can Avoid Fatal Marketing Decisions" panel discussion.

1999
HEMP annual retreat is held at The Elms in Excelsior Springs with special guest speaker Pierre Mornell, Hiring Smart author.

Mentor-Mentee Workshop is held featuring "My Greatest Mistake" panel discussion; among the participants are Barney Karbank, B.A. Karbank & Co.; Rich Davis, KC Masterpiece Barbecue Sauce; and Lirel Holt, U, Inc.

Dean Kopulos and Pierre Mornell at the 1999 HEMP retreat.

2000

HEMP annual retreat is held at The Elms in Excelsior Springs with special guest speaker Jeff Thompson, vice president of PEAK Learning, Inc.

HEMPers participating in an ice breaker activity at the 2000 retreat.

2001

HEMP annual retreat is held at The Fairmont Hotel Kansas City on the Plaza where Ted and Alice Cohn return as retreat speakers.

Celebrate HEMP, an annual event to honor participants and celebrate everything about HEMP, is launched.

Ted and Alice Cohn at the 2001 retreat.

2002

HEMP annual retreat is held at The Fairmont Hotel Kansas City on the Plaza with special guest speakers Fred Lyons of Hoechst Marion Roussel, Inc. and Jerry Haney of Visionomics, Inc.

HEMP's first golf outing and reception takes place at Swope Memorial Golf Course.

2003

HEMP annual retreat is held at The Fairmont Hotel Kansas City on the Plaza with special guest speaker Jeff Comment of Helzberg Diamonds.

The tradition of Schmooze Fest begins at the Helzberg home. Appropriately named, the event is created to give participants a chance to network, or schmooze.

Barnett C. Helzberg, Jr. and Bill Reisler kicking off the first Schmooze Fest in 2003.

2004

HEMP launches its first professional website.

Lunch with The Big Guy meetings start. These are lunches of 6-8 participants sharing a current business challenge with Barnett, The Big Guy.

2005

Ray Pitman creates a new organizational chart to improve HEMP by involving participants in the decision-making.

First formal Mentee graduation ceremony is held during the annual retreat.

Barnett presenting Missy Love with her graduation gift in 2005.

2006

Online Mentee and Mentor training is developed.

Mentee site visits conducted by a large group traveling by limo bus become the new standard.

The HEMP Selection Committee outside the limo at site visits in 2006.

2007

HEMP's newly created Operating System begins documenting all the organization's critical processes.

The Executive Committee is established to act on urgent issues. The committee meets monthly.

2008

HEMP helps Mike Jandernoa launch JEM, Jandernoa Entrepreneurial Mentoring, in Grand Rapids, Michigan.

The graduating Class of 2006's gift, a TV for the HEMP conference room.

2009

HEMP leases office space at 2000 Baltimore Avenue in the Crossroads and moves in.

HEMP receives its first Mentee class gift, a TV for the conference room, presented by the Class of 2006 at their Mentee graduation.

2010

HEMP hosts an open house at its new office space.

2011 - 2012

The *Entrepreneurs + Mentors = Success* book tour takes off at universities in cities such as Witchita, KS and St. Louis, MO.

First State of HEMP event, in which HEMPers have a chance to learn HEMP's plans for the coming year, is held.

2013

HEMP annual retreat is held at The Elms in Excelsior Springs with guest speaker vulnerability researcher Brené Brown.

HEMP hosts its first annual entrepreneurial field trip, kicking off the tradition in Las Vegas with Zappos and Shelby American.

2014

Jacquie Morgan, Sara Croke, Leanne Cofield, and Deborah Young, PhD pose in front of the penguins at the 2014 Schmooze Fest.

HEMP visits Bluebird Café, Tennessee Bun Company, Starstruck Studios, and Dave Ramsey in Nashville.

HEMP refreshes its brand.

Schmooze Fest at the Kansas City Zoo celebrates the opening of the Helzberg Penguin Plaza.

A Restricted Reserve fund is started to ensure the financial stability of HEMP.

2015

HEMP celebrates its twentieth anniversary.

Apple cofounder Steve Wozniak speaks at the annual HEMP retreat.

HEMP visits San Francisco on its annual field trip and tours Praetorian Digital, Tesla, and Salesforce.

All HEMPers are asked to donate an item which represents their business from which a large piece of artwork is created to surprise the Helzbergs for the 20th anniversary.

The Helzbergs receive the special art gift from HEMPers at Celebrate HEMP 2015.

2016

HEMP visits Seattle on its annual field trip. Visits include Starbucks, Amazon, Space Needle and Chihuly Garden and Glass, and Boeing.

HEMP turns twenty-one and becomes legal.

HEMPers at an overlook in Seattle.

2017

HEMP visits Minneapolis on its annual field trip. Tours include Paisley Park, 3M, Medtronic, and The Nerdery.

Barnett debuts his iconic HEMP suit at the annual Celebrate HEMP event.

Shirley is unsure as Barnett debuts his new HEMP suit at Celebrate HEMP in 2017.

Barnett C. Helzberg, Jr.

A Kansas City–area native, Barnett Helzberg, Jr. received a bachelor's degree in business administration from the University of Michigan. He is the former chairman of the board of Helzberg Diamonds (est. 1915) and expanded the company from fifteen units in 1962 into the third-largest jewelry retailer in twenty-three states. In 1995, the company was sold to Berkshire Hathaway (Warren Buffett). Barnett is the creator of the "I Am Loved"® theme and cocreator with Dr. Rich Davis of the book *I Am Loved*®, published in 2001. He is also the author of *What I Learned Before I Sold to Warren Buffett*, published in 2003.

Barnett is currently the chair and founder of the Helzberg Entrepreneurial Mentoring Program and cofounder and board member of the University Academy K–12 Charter School in Kansas City, Missouri. He established the Helzberg Leadership Fellows (a program to train young Jewish leadership) and is also an adjunct professor at Rockhurst University.

Barnett lives with his wife, Shirley. They have two adult sons, Barnett III and Bush, six brilliant grandsons, and one gorgeous and brilliant granddaughter.

Maureen Rank

Maureen Rank is the author or coauthor of more than thirty books. She lives in Kansas City, Missouri.

Tracy Lockton

Tracy Lockton has over 30 years of experience in a variety of entrepreneurial endeavors including software development, technology consulting, buy-outs, and management consulting. She has been a Mentor in HEMP since 2012 and has served on various committees. She has chaired the Mentor committee and served as President.

Christina Dreiling

Christina Dreiling has been with HEMP since 2003 and became the managing director in 2005. She helps HEMP's 225+ entrepreneurs and enjoys "herding the cats."

The Helzberg Entrepreneurial Mentoring Program (HEMP) was founded in 1995 by Barnett Helzberg, Jr., former owner and president of Helzberg Diamonds. Inspired by his twenty-three year mentoring relationship with Ewing Kauffman, HEMP matches seasoned, successful entrepreneur mentors with less-experienced entrepreneur mentees. Considerable mentoring is also fostered through peer-to-peer relationships derived from involvement through HEMP.

Components of the program include a one-on-one mentoring relationship, networking opportunities with peers and veteran business owners, exposure to mentoring skills which can be applied to any professional or personal situation, business education discussing greatest successes and lessons learned from peers and top CEOs in the community, and field trips outside of Kansas City to businesses such as Tesla (San Francisco), Zappos (Las Vegas), Starbucks (Seattle), Dave Ramsey (Nashville), Marel (Iceland) and 3M (Minneapolis).

For more information, contact:
Helzberg Entrepreneurial Mentoring Program (HEMP)
2000 Baltimore Avenue, Suite 200
Kansas City, MO 64108
(816) 471-4367 (HEMP)
info@hempkc.org | www.hempkc.org

www.ingramcontent.com/pod-product-compliance
Lightning Source LLC
Chambersburg PA
CBHW051908210326
41597CB00033B/6068